JOSSEY-BASS TEACHER

Jossey-Bass Teacher provides educators with practical knowledge and tools to create a positive and lifelong impact on student learning. We offer classroom-tested and research-based teaching resources for a variety of grade levels and subject areas. Whether you are an aspiring, new, or veteran teacher, we want to help you make every teaching day your best.

From ready-to-use classroom activities to the latest teaching framework, our value-packed books provide insightful, practical, and comprehensive materials on the topics that matter most to K–12 teachers. We hope to become your trusted source for the best ideas from the most experienced and respected experts in the field.

Other Math Books by the Muschlas

- *Geometry Teacher's Activities Kit: Ready-to-Use Lessons and Worksheets for Grades 6–12*

- *Math Smart! Over 220 Ready-to-Use Activities to Motivate and Challenge Students, Grades 6–12*

- *Algebra Teacher's Activities Kit: 150 Ready-to-Use Activities with Real-World Applications*

- *Math Games: 180 Reproducible Activities to Motivate, Excite, and Challenge Students, Grades 6–12*

- *The Math Teacher's Book of Lists, 2nd Edition*

- *The Math Teacher's Problem-a-Day, Grades 4–8: Over 180 Reproducible Pages of Quick Skill Builders*

- *Hands-On Math Projects with Real-Life Applications, Grades 3–5*

- *Hands-On Math Projects with Real-Life Applications: Grades 6–12, 2nd Edition*

- *Math Teacher's Survival Guide: Practical Strategies, Management Techniques, and Reproducibles for New and Experienced Teachers, Grades 5–12*

- *The Algebra Teacher's Guide to Reteaching Essential Concepts and Skills: 150 Mini-Lessons for Correcting Common Mistakes*

- *Math Starters: 5- to 10-Minute Activities Aligned with the Common Core Math Standards, Grades 6–12, 2nd Edition*

- *Teaching the Common Core Math Standards with Hands-On Activities, Grades 6–8*

- *Teaching the Common Core Math Standards with Hands-On Activities, Grades 3–5*

Teaching the Common Core Math Standards with Hands-On Activities, Grades K–2

Judith A. Muschla

Gary Robert Muschla

Erin Muschla-Berry

JB JOSSEY-BASS™

A Wiley Brand

Published by Jossey-Bass
A Wiley Brand
One Montgomery Street, Suite 1200, San Francisco, CA 94101–4594—www.josseybass.com

Jossey-Bass books and products are available through most bookstores. To contact Jossey-Bass directly call our Customer Care Department within the U.S. at 800-956-7739, outside the U.S. at 317-572-3986, or fax 317-572-4002.

Wiley publishes in a variety of print and electronic formats and by print-on-demand. Some material included with standard print versions of this book may not be included in e-books or in print-on-demand. If this book refers to media such as a CD or DVD that is not included in the version you purchased, you may download this material at http://booksupport.wiley.com. For more information about Wiley products, visit www.wiley.com.

Library of Congress Cataloging-in-Publication Data
Muschla, Judith A., author.
    Teaching the common core math standards with hands-on activities, grades K-2 / Judith A. Muschla, Gary Robert Muschla, Erin Muschla-Berry.
        pages cm. — (Jossey-Bass teacher)
    Includes index.
    ISBN 978-1-118-71024-1 (paperback); ISBN 978-1-118-71016-6 (ebook); ISBN 978-1-118-93163-9 (ebook)
    1. Mathematics—Study and teaching (Preschool)—Standards—United States. 2. Mathematics—Study and teaching (Primary)—Standards—United States. 3. Mathematics—Study and teaching (Preschool)—Activity programs—United States. 4. Mathematics—Study and teaching (Primary)—Activity programs—United States.   I. Muschla, Gary Robert, author. II. Muschla-Berry, Erin, author. III. Title.
    QA135.6.M874 2014
    372.7′049—dc23
                                                                                                    2014010408

Printed in the United States of America

FIRST EDITION

PB Printing   10 9 8 7 6 5 4 3 2 1

ABOUT THIS BOOK

The Common Core State Standards Initiative for Mathematics identifies the concepts, skills, and practices that students should understand and apply at their grade level. Mastery of these Standards at the primary level will provide students with the basic concepts and skills essential for future success in math.

Teaching the Common Core Math Standards with Hands-On Activities, Grades K–2 offers a variety of activities that support instruction of the Standards. The Table of Contents, which contains a complete list of Standards and supporting activities for these grades, is divided into three sections:

- Section 1: Standards and Activities for Kindergarten

- Section 2: Standards and Activities for Grade 1

- Section 3: Standards and Activities for Grade 2

The book is designed for easy implementation. The activities build on concepts and skills that you have already taught and expand the scope of your instruction through reinforcement and enrichment. Each activity is preceded by the Domain, which is a group of related Standards, followed by the specific Standard that the activity addresses. For example, "Operations and Algebraic Thinking: 1.OA.2" refers to the Domain, which is Operations and Algebraic Thinking, Grade 1, and Standard 2. Next comes background information on the topic, the title and a brief summary of the activity, special materials needed for the activity, and any special preparation that is necessary. Icons highlight activities that include cooperative learning, 👪, or that incorporate the use of technology, 💻. All of the activities include specific steps for implementation, and many include reproducibles.

At least one activity supports every Standard for kindergarten through second grade. The typical activity can be completed in one class period and focuses on application of concepts or skills, demonstration of understanding, or communication about math. Students may be required to solve problems, create mathematical models, conduct investigations with manipulatives, play mathematical games, or explain their reasoning. While many of the activities are open-ended, answer keys are provided for those that require specific answers.

Because many of the activities may be developed through various methods, we encourage you to modify them in ways that best meet the needs of your students. For example, rather than presenting an activity in one session, you might decide to present it in two or three. In some activities where we suggest that students work in pairs or groups of three, you may feel that your students will gain the most from the activity by working individually. Conversely, for some activities, instead of having students work individually, you may find it more practical to have them work with a partner. For some activities that require the use of special materials, spinners for instance, you may substitute another item, such as dice. You should present each activity in a manner that meets your objectives, is appropriate for your students, and is easy for you to manage.

To enhance your instruction of the activities in this book, consider the following:

- Use a variety of instructional tools, such as traditional boards, whiteboards, overhead projectors, document cameras, computers, and digital projectors to present material in an effective and interesting manner.

- Use manipulatives, both physical and virtual, and materials that provide hands-on experiences to enhance the learning process.

- Preview every Web site and work through any exercises so that you are better able to offer guidance during the actual activity. Also, place the URLs of Web sites in your browser to make the Web site easy to access.

- For activities that require cutting out cards, consider enlarging the cards, copying them on card stock, and laminating them to preserve them for future use.

- For activities that include games for students to play, provide a prize or a homework pass to the winners.

We hope that the activities in this resource prove to be both interesting and enjoyable for you and your students, and that the activities help your students master the math concepts and skills of the Standards at your grade level. We extend to you our best wishes for a successful and rewarding year.

Judith A. Muschla
Gary Robert Muschla
Erin Muschla-Berry

ABOUT THE AUTHORS

Judith A. Muschla received her BA in Mathematics from Douglass College at Rutgers University and is certified to teach K–12. She taught mathematics in South River, New Jersey, for over twenty-five years at various levels at both South River High School and South River Middle School. As a team leader at the middle school, she wrote several math curriculums, coordinated interdisciplinary units, and conducted mathematics workshops for teachers and parents. She also served as a member of the state Review Panel for New Jersey's Mathematics Core Curriculum Content Standards.

Together, Judith and Gary Muschla have coauthored several math books published by Jossey-Bass: *Hands-On Math Projects with Real-Life Applications, Grades 3–5* (2009); *The Math Teacher's Problem-a-Day, Grades 4–8* (2008); *Hands-On Math Projects with Real-Life Applications, Grades 6–12* (1996; second edition, 2006); *The Math Teacher's Book of Lists* (1995; second edition, 2005); *Math Games: 180 Reproducible Activities to Motivate, Excite, and Challenge Students, Grades 6–12* (2004); *Algebra Teacher's Activities Kit* (2003); *Math Smart! Over 220 Ready-to-Use Activities to Motivate and Challenge Students, Grades 6–12* (2002); *Geometry Teacher's Activities Kit* (2000); and *Math Starters! 5- to 10-Minute Activities to Make Kids Think, Grades 6–12* (1999).

Gary Robert Muschla received his BA and MAT from Trenton State College and taught in Spotswood, New Jersey, for more than twenty-five years at the elementary school level. He is a successful author and a member of the Authors Guild and the National Writers Association. In addition to math resources, he has written several resources for English and writing teachers, among them *Writing Workshop Survival Kit* (1993; second edition, 2005); *The Writing Teacher's Book of Lists* (1991; second edition, 2004); *Ready-to-Use Reading Proficiency Lessons and Activities, 10th Grade Level* (2003); *Ready-to-Use Reading Proficiency Lessons and Activities, 8th Grade Level* (2002); *Ready-to-Use Reading Proficiency Lessons and Activities, 4th Grade Level* (2002); *Reading Workshop Survival Kit* (1997); and *English Teacher's Great Books Activities Kit* (1994), all published by Jossey-Bass.

Erin Muschla-Berry received her BS and MEd from The College of New Jersey. She is certified to teach grades K–8 with Mathematics Specialization in Grades 5–8. She currently teaches math at Monroe Township Middle School in Monroe, New Jersey, and has presented workshops for math teachers for the Association of Mathematics Teachers of New Jersey. She has coauthored six books with Judith and Gary Muschla for Jossey-Bass: *Teaching the Common Core Math Standards with Hands-On Activities, Grades 3–5* (2014); *Math Starters, 2nd Edition: 5- to 10-Minute Activities Aligned with the Common Core Standards, Grades 6–12* (2013); *Teaching the Common Core Math Standards with Hands-On Activities, Grades 6–8* (2012); *The Algebra Teacher's Guide to Reteaching Essential Concepts and Skills* (2011); *The Elementary Teacher's Book of Lists* (2010); and *Math Teacher's Survival Guide, Grades 5–12* (2010).

ACKNOWLEDGMENTS

We thank Jeff Corey Gorman, EdD, assistant superintendent of Monroe Township Public Schools, Chari Chanley, EdS, principal of Monroe Township Middle School, James Higgins, vice principal of Monroe Township Middle School, and Scott Sidler, vice principal of Monroe Township Middle School, for their support.

We also thank Kate Bradford, our editor at Jossey-Bass, for her guidance and suggestions on yet another book.

Special thanks to Diane Turso, our proofreader, for helping to finalize this book.

We appreciate the support of our many colleagues who, over the years, have encouraged us in our work.

And, of course, we wish to acknowledge the many students we have had the satisfaction of teaching.

CONTENTS

Standards and Activities for Kindergarten

Counting and Cardinality: K.CC.1

"Know number names and the count sequence."

> 1. "Count to 100 by ones and by tens."

BACKGROUND

When young children are learning to count, they may count some numbers more than once, skip numbers, and count numbers in the wrong order. Such instances are signs that they do not think of numbers as having any specific order or any relationship to other numbers. To count accurately, children need to understand that numbers are related to other numbers and that order matters.

ACTIVITY 1: READING A COUNTING BOOK

The teacher reads *Richard Scarry's Best Counting Book Ever* to the class and discusses numbers and counting.

MATERIALS

Richard Scarry's Best Counting Book Ever by Richard Scarry (Sterling, 2010).

PROCEDURE

1. Gather your students around you so that you will be able to share the illustrations with them as you read. Explain that you are going to read a book about Willy Bunny and counting.

2. As you read, pause often and encourage your students to count along with the story. Show the illustrations that will help them to associate numbers with objects.

3. Explain the order of the numbers. For example, 1 comes before 2 and $1 + 1$ makes 2; 2 comes before 3 and $2 + 1$ makes 3; 3 comes before 4 and $3 + 1$ makes 4; and so on. Explain that 10 ones make 10, and that groups of 10 make 20, 30, and so on.

CLOSURE

Discuss the book with your students and review the relationships between numbers. Ask your students to recall numbers and relate them to objects in the book. Turn to specific pages to reinforce numbers and objects.

ACTIVITY 2: COUNTING FLOOR TILES

This activity may be divided into sessions over a few days. Students count off tiles as they walk, first by ones and then by tens.

MATERIALS

A floor with at least 100 tiles; for example, a hallway or gymnasium floor.

PROCEDURE

1. Explain to your students that they will count to 100, using floor tiles as a guide.

2. Take your students into the hallway or gym, or similar area where the floor is covered with tiles. Select a place that will not disturb others as your students count.

3. You may conduct the activity by having your students follow each other in a long line and walk on the same tiles, or you may divide them into groups and have them walk along tiles in separate lines.

4. To begin the activity, instruct your students to step forward, one tile at a time, and as a group count in order: 1, 2, 3, … 100. You may count with them, your voice serving as a guide. If necessary, correct students to ensure that they count accurately. Repeat this activity a few times to make certain that all your students understand the sequence of counting to 100. An option here is to have your students count tiles (quietly, of course) as they walk through the halls to gym, art, music, or other special classes.

5. After counting to 100 as a class, explain to your students that they will now count by tens to 100. (Note: You may prefer to complete this part of the activity on another day.) Lead the class in counting by tens so that all students know what they are to do. Depending on the abilities of your students, you may explain that 10 is a group of 10 ones; 20, therefore, is made up of two groups of 10 ones, or 2 tens, and other tens are similarly made up of groups of 10 ones.

6. Working as a whole class, or in groups, have your students walk and count tiles by tens. They should silently count by ones and then say every interval of 10.

CLOSURE

Upon returning to class, discuss that counting by ones from 1 to 100 includes some of the same numbers as when counting by tens from 10 to 100 (the multiples of ten). Ask your students to name these numbers. For reinforcement, and also to allow you to check for understanding, have groups of students count while you listen.

ACTIVITY 3: PASS THE CRITTER AND COUNT

Sitting in a circle, students pass a stuffed animal from one student to another and count from 1 to 100. The first student says 1, the second student says 2, the third students says 3, and the procedure continues to 100. After counting by ones, students pass the critter in the same fashion and count by tens from 10 to 100.

MATERIALS

A small stuffed animal.

PROCEDURE

1. Have your students sit in a circle, either on the floor or in their chairs.

2. Introduce the stuffed animal who will help them count. Explain that they will pass the stuffed animal along, from one student to another, and count. Upon receiving the stuffed animal, each student will say the number that follows the number that the student before her said, and then pass the stuffed animal to the next student who says the next number. The class will count from 1 to 100. Encourage your students to count silently to themselves as the stuffed animal is passed, as this will help to reinforce the counting sequence for them. Correct students if they make mistakes in counting. (A variation of this exercise is to allow students to pass the stuffed animal to whomever they wish. In this case, you must make sure that every student gets a chance to count and that some students do not get significantly more chances than others.)

3. After students have counted by ones to 100, repeat the activity by having them pass the stuffed animal around and count by tens to 100.

CLOSURE

Lead the class in counting by ones to 100 and then in counting by tens to 100. Ask for volunteers to count by tens from 10 to 100.

Counting and Cardinality: K.CC.2

"Know number names and the count sequence."

2. "Count forward beginning from a given number within the known sequence (instead of having to begin at 1)."

BACKGROUND

Cardinal numbers, such as 1, 12, and 57, indicate quantity. A cardinal number does not indicate order. Only when we count do cardinal numbers become part of a sequence.

 ### ACTIVITY 1: PICK A NUMBER AND COUNT

Working in groups, students draw a card from two separate sets of cards. Each card in the first set contains a number from 1 to 9. Each card in the second set contains a number from 0 to 9. Together, the numbers on the cards will form a two-digit number, from which students are to count to 100.

MATERIALS

Reproducibles, "Number Set, I" and "Number Set, II," for each group of students; scissors or paper cutter for the teacher.

PREPARATION

Make 1 copy of each reproducible for each group. (Copying each reproducible on a different color of paper will make it easy to keep the two sets of cards separate. It will also allow you to make a distinction between tens and ones, should you choose to reinforce this concept.) After making copies, cut the cards out but keep the sets separate so that you may give one of each set to each group.

PROCEDURE

1. Distribute both sets of number cards to each group. Caution students to keep the cards in separate piles, with the numbers from "Number Set, I" being in the first pile and the numbers from "Number Set, II" being in the second pile. Note that the second pile should contain a zero.

2. Instruct your students to turn the two sets of cards face down and mix up the cards in each set. One student then picks a number from each set. Explain that the first card should be

selected from the first pile and represents the first number of a two-digit number (or the tens), and the second card, picked from the second pile, represents the second number (or the ones.) The two-digit number made up of both cards is the number that the group starts counting from as they count to 100. For example, if the first card picked was 5 and the second was 8, the group would start counting from 58. You may want to point out that the number 6 and the number 9 are underlined. Ask your students why this might be. Even at this age students might realize that the underlining is to make sure that the numbers are not mistakenly turned upside down so that the 6 and 9 are misread.

3. Explain that the student who picked the cards should place them aside and then start counting by saying the number. The other students in the group follow, one after the other, each student stating the next number in sequence, counting until they reach 100. As a student states a number, if a member of the group believes that the number is incorrect, he should raise his hand. The counting sequence stops and the group members discuss what the next number should be. You should then verify that the number they agree on is correct, and the counting sequence continues.

4. Explain that after counting to 100, another student in the group chooses two new cards, one from each set. The two-digit number made from the numbers on the cards is the new starting number and the counting exercise is repeated. The activity goes on until all group members pick numbers. If time remains, you may have students do another round.

CLOSURE

Discuss some of the numbers groups counted from. Ask questions such as the following: Which, if any, numbers did you find to be harder to count from than others? Which numbers, if any, were easiest to count from? Why?

ACTIVITY 2: A RANDOM NUMBER GENERATOR

The teacher uses a random number generator from a Web site to generate numbers from 1–100. Students will count from the generated number to 100.

MATERIALS

Computer with Internet access; digital projector for the teacher.

PROCEDURE

1. Explain to your students that a random number generator is a computer program that finds numbers in no particular order. A person cannot know what the number will be until it appears.

2. Go to http://www.random.org and project the Web site onto a screen. (Note: There are many Web sites that have random number generators; a simple search with the term "random number generator" will list several.)

3. Once at the Web site, enter a 1 for "Min" and 100 for "Max." Click on "Generate" and the program will generate a number randomly between 1 and 100.

4. Announce the number to your students. You may have the class, together, count from the number to 100, or you may instead call on a student, ask her to count the next five numbers, then call on another student to count the next five and so on until the count reaches 100. Correct students, if necessary, as they count.

5. After counting to 100 from the first number, generate another number and repeat the exercise. Continue the process with more numbers.

CLOSURE

Still using the random number generator, generate numbers and ask volunteers to count the next ten numbers (or the next numbers to 100 if the generated number is 91 or more). You may find it helpful to prompt students to stop counting at the tenth number.

1	2
3	4
5	6
7	8
9	

0	1
2	3
4	5
6	7
8	9

Counting and Cardinality: K.CC.3

"Know number names and the count sequence."

> 3. "Write numbers from 0 to 20. Represent a number of objects with a written numeral 0–20 (with 0 representing a count of no objects)."

BACKGROUND

Representing numbers with objects provides children with visual models. Such models help children to recognize a quantitative difference between numbers. For example, 2 is clearly represented by fewer objects than 9, and 9 is represented by fewer objects than 10. Representing numbers with objects can also help children understand that when counting, each number is 1 more than the number preceding it.

ACTIVITY 1: MINIATURE MATH BINGO

Students receive a bingo board on which they will randomly write the numbers 0 to 20. As the teacher says a number, students find the number on their bingo board and cover it with a counter. The first student to cover five squares in a row, column, or along a diagonal wins.

MATERIALS

25 counters; reproducible, "Miniature Math Bingo," for each student.

PROCEDURE

1. Explain that students are to play a game called bingo. But this game is a little different from the standard game of bingo. In this game, students will match numbers that you call with numbers on their boards.

2. Hand out the materials. Explain that the "Miniature Math Bingo" board contains spaces and free spaces. At the bottom of the board is the Number Bank, with numbers from 0 to 20. Students are to randomly write each number in a space on their board, except the free spaces. Be sure to explain that "randomly" means no special order. As they write a number in a space, they should cross it out on the bottom of the page so that they do not mistakenly use it again. All numbers will be used.

3. After students have written numbers in the spaces, instruct them to place one counter on each of the four free spaces.

4. Explain the rules of the game. You will call out a number from 0 to 20, which you will select from a list. You may create your own list or use the following one: 9, 0, 13, 5, 11, 19, 2, 16, 14, 10, 3, 7, 20, 17, 6, 18, 12, 4, 1, 15, and 8. As you say a number, students are to find the number on their bingo board and place a counter on its space. The first student who has five spaces covered in a row, column, or along a diagonal is the winner. (Be sure your students understand what "row," "column," and "diagonal" mean.) The student should raise his hand and say "Bingo!" Check his answers to make certain that they are correct. If, after you have announced all of the numbers, there is no winner, you may declare the student who has the most consecutively covered numbers in a row, column, or along a diagonal the winner. (There may be more than one winner.) Play more games by presenting the numbers in a different order.

CLOSURE

Discuss the game. Ask your students if anyone else was close to getting bingo. If yes, what number, or numbers, did they yet need?

ACTIVITY 2: NUMBERS AND OBJECTS

Students are given the numbers 0 to 20, one at a time. They are to use counters to represent the numbers and then write each number and draw objects to represent it. (Note: You may prefer to divide this activity into two or three sessions.)

MATERIALS

20 counters; crayons; unlined paper for each student.

PROCEDURE

1. Hand out the materials. Explain that students will use the counters to represent numbers. They will then write the numbers and draw objects to represent the numbers on unlined paper.

2. Start with 0. Ask your students how many objects are represented by zero. Because zero represents no objects, instruct your students to write 0 on their unlined paper without any objects because zero means none.

3. Say the number 1. Ask your students to use their counters to represent 1. Scan the counters to check that students are correct before you move on. After they show 1 with one counter, they should write the numeral 1 on their paper and then draw one object to represent 1. Objects need not be complicated; dots, circles, squares, and so on are fine. Students may color their objects.

4. Say the number 2 and instruct your students to follow the same procedure. They should first represent the numeral with counters. Then they should write the numeral and draw objects that represent it on their unlined paper. Give your students time to work and then move on to the number 3. You should have students draw objects to represent all of the numbers from 0 to 20.

CLOSURE

Have students share their work with a partner. It is likely that students used different objects to represent numbers. Explain that although the objects may be different, the number of objects that represent a particular number should be the same. Display the work of your students.

Bingo Board				
	Free Space			
				Free Space
Free Space				
			Free Space	

Number Bank

0	1	2	3	4	5	6
7	8	9	10	11	12	13
14	15	16	17	18	19	20

Counting and Cardinality: K.CC.4

"Count to tell the number of objects."

4. "Understand the relationship between numbers and quantities; connect counting to cardinality.

   a. "When counting objects, say the number names in the standard order, pairing each object with one and only one number name and each number name with one and only one object.

   b. "Understand that the last number name said tells the number of objects counted. The number of objects is the same regardless of their arrangement or the order in which they were counted.

   c. "Understand that each successive number name refers to a quantity that is one larger."

BACKGROUND

When children realize the connection between counting numbers and the quantities those numbers represent, they begin to understand numbers in terms of order, sequence, and value. They recognize that when counting, each number is one more than the number that came before it and one less than the number that comes after it.

 ### ACTIVITY 1: PAIRING NUMBERS AND OBJECTS

Working in pairs or groups of three, students will be given 20 cards with pictures of objects that represent numbers. Students will create a poster by writing the numbers 1 to 20 on construction paper and gluing each card next to its matching number. Students will share their work with the class.

MATERIALS

Glue sticks; crayons; large white construction paper; reproducibles, "Numbers-Objects Cards, I" and "Numbers-Objects Cards, II," for each pair or group of students; scissors or paper cutter for the teacher.

PREPARATION

Make 1 copy of each reproducible for each pair or group of students. (Each reproducible contains object cards representing ten numbers. Together, the reproducibles contain object cards representing the numbers from 1 to 20.) Cut out the individual object cards from the reproducibles, being careful to keep each set of object cards from 1 to 20 separate. Note that the objects are not in numerical order. Optional: A poster you create as an example for your students.

PROCEDURE

1. Hand out the materials. Explain that the 20 object cards represent the numbers from 1 to 20. The cards are not in numerical order.

2. Explain that students are to first arrange the cards in the correct sequence, 1 to 20. After arranging the cards in order, students are to write the numbers, 1 to 20, on their construction paper. Suggest how your students might write the numbers on their posters—perhaps going across the paper from left to right, or up and down, leaving enough space between numbers so that they have room to place an object card next to each number. If you created a poster of your own, show it to your students as an example.

3. After students have written the numbers on their paper, explain that they are to glue each object card next to its matching number. Suggest that students color the objects.

CLOSURE

Check your students' posters and have them share their posters with the class. They might simply stand by their seats and hold their posters up. To reinforce number names, have a volunteer from each pair or group recite the numbers on their posters. Perhaps partners or the members of a group would like to say the numbers together. Be sure to discuss that a specific number of objects—no matter what the objects are—always represents the same number. Display your students' posters.

ACTIVITY 2: FILLING IN NUMBERS AND OBJECTS

Students will complete a worksheet on which they must write missing numbers and supply missing objects.

MATERIALS

Crayons; reproducible, "Missing Numbers and Objects," for each student.

PROCEDURE

1. Hand out the materials. Explain that the reproducible contains four lines of numbers; each line of numbers is written in order, but the lines do not follow each other sequentially. Below each number are objects in the form of darkened circles that represent the number. But some numbers and objects in the line are missing.

2. Explain that students are to write the missing numbers in the blank spaces and draw the correct number of objects that represent them.

3. Do the first missing number in the first line as an example. Ask your students: What is the first missing number? They should realize that 3 is missing. Instruct them to write the numeral 3 in the space between 2 and 4. Ask: How many objects should you draw below the 3? Students should realize that they should draw 3 objects. Suggest that they draw 3 small darkened circles with a crayon. Students are to finish the worksheet in the same manner.

CLOSURE

Discuss students' results. Ask for volunteers to provide the missing numbers in each row. Also discuss that each number is one more than the number before it. For example, in the first line, 3 is one more than 2, 4 is one more than 3, and 5 is one more than 4.

ANSWERS

Note that the objects beneath each number should equal the number. **(1)** 3, 5 **(2)** 12, 14 **(3)** 7, 8 **(4)** 18, 20

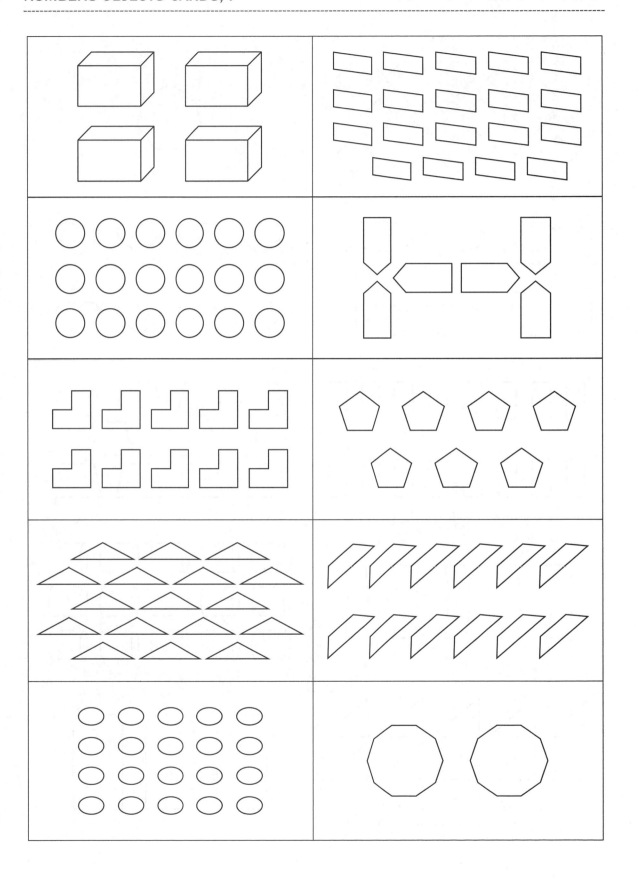

MISSING NUMBERS AND OBJECTS

Directions: Fill in each space with the missing numbers. Draw objects that show each missing number.

1)   1   2   _____   4   _____

2)   11   _____   13   _____   15

3)   6   _____   _____   9   10

4)   16   17   _____   19   _____

Counting and Cardinality: K.CC.5

"Count to tell the number of objects."

> 5. "Count to answer 'how many?' questions about as many as 20 things arranged in a line, a rectangular array, or a circle, or as many as 10 things in a scattered configuration; given a number from 1–20, count out that many objects."

BACKGROUND

Using objects to represent numbers when counting can help children recognize the relationship between counting and quantity. This naturally leads to the question of "how many?"

 ACTIVITY 1: COUNTING OUT

Working in groups, students will each receive a small cup containing up to 20 objects. (The numbers of objects in the cups will vary.) Students are to individually count the objects in their cup, and then record their results using a number and a drawing. They are to then check how many objects the other members of their group found.

MATERIALS

1 small plastic cup (or similar container); enough objects—perhaps counters, buttons, paperclips, and so on—to fill each cup with between 9 and 20 objects; crayons; 1 sheet of unlined paper for each student.

PREPARATION

Fill plastic cups—1 for each student—with one kind of object but with varying numbers of objects. For example, one student's cup might have 9 paperclips, another student's cup might have 13 counters, and a third student's cup might have 18 buttons. No cup should contain more than 20 objects.

PROCEDURE

1. Hand out the materials. Explain that each student's cup contains a number of one kind of object. The number of objects in the cups varies from student to student in each group.

2. Explain that students are to count the number of objects in their cups. Suggest that they arrange the objects in a line to make them easier to count.

3. After they are finished counting, they are to write the number of objects on their paper and then draw and color the correct number of objects.

4. After students have finished drawing their objects, ask them to compare how many objects each member of the group counted. (You may want to emphasize the question "How many?") They should also share their drawings.

CLOSURE

Ask the members of each group to report how many objects they counted. Who, in each group, counted the most? Who counted the least?

ACTIVITY 2: TOSS THE DIE

Each student receives a container that has 20 objects. Each student tosses 1 die and then counts out the number of objects that equals the number on his or her die. Each student rolls the die three times and records his or her results.

MATERIALS

1 die (with the numbers 1–6); a plastic cup (or similar container); 20 objects, such as counters, beads, or buttons for each cup; crayons; unlined paper for each student.

PREPARATION

Fill each cup with 20 objects.

PROCEDURE

1. Hand out the materials.
2. Explain that students are to toss their die. They are to count out the same number of objects from their cup as the number that appears on their die. For example, if they rolled a 4, they must count out 4 objects from their cup. They are to record their results by writing a number and drawing the objects on their paper. They are to toss their die two more times, counting out a matching number of objects for each toss and recording their results two more times. Suggest that students color the objects they draw.
3. Explain that after the third time, they are to count up the total number of objects they rolled (for all three times). They should record this number and draw objects to represent it on their paper.

CLOSURE

Discuss students' results. Ask for volunteers to explain the numbers they rolled and the objects they took from their cup with the first roll of their die, the second, and the third. Ask: Who had the highest number after the first roll? After the second? After the third? Who had the highest number after counting all three rolls together? Who had the lowest number?

Counting and Cardinality: K.CC.6

"Compare numbers."

> 6. "Identify whether the number of objects in one group is greater than, less than, or equal to the number of objects in another group, e.g., by using matching and counting strategies."

BACKGROUND

A significant step in understanding numbers occurs when children are able to recognize when the number of one group of objects is greater than, less than, or equal to the number of objects of another group. Once children make this connection, they are able to compare numbers and the quantities the numbers represent.

 ACTIVITY: COMPARING OBJECTS AND NUMBERS

Working in pairs or groups of three, students will each be given a suit from a standard deck of playing cards, from ace (representing 1) to 10. They will each mix their suits of cards up, pick one card, and then compare the objects on their cards to the objects on their partner's card to find which is larger, smaller, or if the cards are equal. Students will individually record their results.

MATERIALS

1 suit of standard playing cards, ace to 10; reproducible, "Comparing Numbers," for each student.

PREPARATION

Select the ace through 10 cards from standard decks of playing cards. Each student should have his or her own suit of cards.

PROCEDURE

1. Hand out the materials. (Providing students who are working together with suits of different colors will help them to keep their sets of cards separate.) Instruct students to mix up the cards, but be sure to keep each suit separate.

2. Instruct your students to each pick one card from their suits at a time. They are to compare the objects on their cards—hearts, spades, diamonds, or clubs—by counting the objects

to find which card has the greater number of objects. Point out that the number of objects they count on each card should be the same as the number on the card.

3. After they compare the two cards, explain that students are to record their results on their reproducible, writing the number of the objects on their cards in the correct spaces. For example, assume the first card Student A picks is 7 and the first card Student B picks is 3. Student A will fill in the blanks for his first "is greater than" statement—7 is greater than 3. Student B will fill in the blanks for his first "is less than" statement—3 is less than 7. If the cards are equal, both students fill in an "is equal to" statement. Make sure that students understand the terms "is greater than," "is less than," and "is equal to." Note that not all spaces on their reproducibles will be filled. However, depending on the comparisons, students may need another sheet to record all their results. (For groups of three, consider this procedure: Student A and Student B pick and compare cards and then record their results. Student C and Student A pick, compare, and record their cards. Student C and B pick, compare, and record their cards. The exercise continues in this way until no cards are left.)

4. After students have used all of their cards, you may instruct them to mix their cards up again and repeat the exercise.

CLOSURE

Discuss your students' results. Ask questions such as the following: Who picked the most "greater than" cards? Who picked the most "less than" cards? How many times did you and your partner pick cards that were equal? In each case, students should provide examples.

COMPARING NUMBERS

Directions: Compare the numbers of objects and fill in the blanks.

_____ is greater than _____.　　_____ is less than _____.

_____ is greater than _____.　　_____ is less than _____.

_____ is greater than _____.　　_____ is less than _____.

_____ is greater than _____.　　_____ is less than _____.

_____ is greater than _____.　　_____ is less than _____.

_____ is greater than _____.　　_____ is less than _____.

_____ is equal to _____.　　_____ is equal to _____.

_____ is equal to _____.　　_____ is equal to _____.

Counting and Cardinality: K.CC.7

"Compare numbers."

> 7. "Compare two numbers between 1 and 10 presented as written numerals."

BACKGROUND

Recognizing that a number is greater than, less than, or equal to another number—without having to count objects that represent the numbers—indicates that children have begun to acquire number sense. They no longer view a number as merely representing a specific quantity, but understand the quantity represented by a number in relation to quantities represented by other numbers.

 ACTIVITY: COMPARING NUMBERS

Working in pairs or groups of three, students will use a spinner to generate numbers that they will compare. They will individually record their results.

MATERIALS

1 spinner with the numbers 1 to 10 for each pair or group of students (number cards, without objects on them, can be substituted for spinners); reproducible, "Comparing Numbers," found in the activity for Standard K.CC.6 for each student.

PREPARATION

Because spinners usually are not available with the numbers 1 through 10, you may need to alter spinners with the numbers 0 through 9 by writing a 1 before the 0 to make 10. (Note: If you prefer to make spinners of your own, many online sites offer instructions. A search using a phrase such as "making a spinner for the classroom" will result in helpful Web sites.)

PROCEDURE

1. Hand out the spinners to each pair or group of students and a copy of the reproducible to each student.

2. Explain that each student is to spin the spinner and then compare the numbers, finding which number is greater than, less than, or equal to the other.

3. Instruct your students to record their results after each spin on their reproducible. They should write whether the number they spun was greater than, less than, or equal to the number spun by their partner. Make sure that students understand the terms "is greater than," "is less than," and "is equal to" on the reproducible. (For groups of three, consider this procedure: Student A and Student B spin and compare numbers and then record their results. Student C and Student A spin, compare, and record their numbers. Student C and B spin, compare, and record their numbers. The exercise continues in this way.)

4. Instruct your students to spin at least 10 times each and compare 10 pairs of numbers. Note that not all spaces on the reproducible will be filled. However, depending on the comparisons, they may need another sheet to record all their results.

CLOSURE

Discuss students' comparisons. Have volunteers give examples of some numbers that were greater than others, some that were less than others, and some that were equal. Ask your students: Why do you think other students had different results from yours?

Operations and Algebraic Thinking: K.OA.1

"Understand addition as putting together and adding to, and understand subtraction as taking apart and taking from."

> 1. "Represent addition and subtraction with objects, fingers, mental images, drawings, sounds (e.g., claps), acting out situations, verbal explanations, expressions, or equations."

BACKGROUND

Before children can add or subtract, they must realize that addition is a process of putting together and adding to and that subtraction is a process of taking apart and taking from. Representing addition and subtraction with objects, drawings, and equations can help students acquire this fundamental understanding.

 ACTIVITY 1: REPRESENTING ADDITION AND SUBTRACTION

This is a two-day activity. The first day focuses on addition and the second day focuses on subtraction. Working in pairs or groups of three, students will roll dice to make addition and subtraction problems, and then represent each problem with counters, a drawing, and an equation.

MATERIALS

1 die; 12 counters; crayons for each pair or group of students; reproducibles, "Addition Equations" and "Subtraction Equations," for each student.

PROCEDURE

Day One

1. Hand out the materials to each pair or group of students and a copy of the reproducible "Addition Equations" to each student. Explain that the reproducible contains blank spaces for numbers that will make equations for ten addition problems. As they complete the activity, each student will fill in the spaces on his or her own sheet with numbers.

2. Explain that addition is the process of putting numbers together or adding one number to another number. Provide an example that models $2 + 3$ using counters. Start with 2 counters and then add 3 counters for a sum of 5 counters.

3. Explain the activity and do the first addition equation on the reproducible together as a class. Ask a volunteer to throw a die. Now ask another volunteer to throw a die. Explain

that using counters, the students are to represent the numbers that appear face up on their die. For example, assume that the first student threw a 4 and the second student threw a 1. The numbers can be represented by 4 counters and by 1 counter, respectively. By combining and counting the counters, students can find the sum of the two numbers, which is 5. They are to then use these numbers to complete the first addition equation on their reproducible, writing 4 in the first blank, 1 in the second blank, and 5 in the third blank. After they have written the numbers in the correct spaces, they are to draw and color objects—small circles, squares, or simple check marks—under each number. Students are to follow this process for all of the addition problems. (For groups of three, Student A and Student B both throw a die for the first problem. For the second problem, Student C throws a die with Student A throwing the second die. For the next problem, Student C throws a die with Student B throwing the second die. Students take turns in this fashion.)

Day Two

1. Hand out the materials to each pair or group of students and a copy of the reproducible "Subtraction Equations" to each student. Explain that the reproducible contains blank spaces for numbers that will make equations for ten subtraction problems. As they complete the activity, each student will fill in the spaces on his or her own sheet with numbers.

2. Explain that subtraction is the process of taking apart or taking a number away from an equal or larger number. Provide an example that models 4 − 1. Start with 4 counters and then take away 1 counter, leaving 3 counters.

3. Explain how students are to complete the subtraction problems. Students are to each toss one die. In subtraction, because they will be taking a smaller number away from an equal or larger number, students must begin the equation with the larger number that appears on the dice. For example, if the first student tossed a 3 and the second student tossed a 5, students must start the equation with the 5. (If the two numbers tossed are equal, it does not matter whose number they start with.) Students should represent the problem with counters. In the example of tossing a 3 and 5, they would count out 5 counters and then take 3 counters away from the 5, leaving 2 counters, which is the difference. After they have represented their problem with counters, students are to record their results on their reproducible and complete the equation. They are to draw the larger group of objects (for example, 5 circles) and then cross out the number of objects that are being subtracted (for example, 3 circles). They may then color the remaining objects (for example, 2 circles).

CLOSURE

Discuss your students' results. Ask for volunteers to share some of the equations they wrote. Review the fact that addition is a process of putting numbers together or adding one number to another, and that subtraction is a process of taking apart or taking a number away from an equal or larger number.

ACTIVITY 2: MINI-MATH SKIT

Working in groups, students will act out mini-scenes that represent addition and subtraction.

MATERIALS

Scissors or paper cutter; one copy of reproducible, "Ideas for Mini-Math Skits."

PREPARATION

Make one copy of the reproducible. Cut out the six scenes, one scene for each group of students. Note that numbers are not included in the scenes. You may write in numbers so that the numbers of characters in each scene match the number of students in the group. You may, of course, add your own scenes to this activity.

PROCEDURE

1. Explain that each group will act out a short skit that represents addition or subtraction.

2. Hand out a skit to each group and explain the skit that each group receives.

3. Explain that students are to think about how they may act out the scene to show addition or subtraction. Here is an example for a group of four students acting out a scene that shows addition: Two birds are sitting on a tree limb and two more birds join them. Students can act this out by having two students sit on a desk or table (tree limb), and two other students flap their arms (wings) and join them.

4. Provide a few minutes for students to brainstorm ideas. It is likely you will need to provide some guidance and suggestions to the groups. Visit with each group and ask them about their skit. What will they do? What role will each student play? Encourage students to use their imaginations.

CLOSURE

Introduce each skit to the class and have each group perform their mini-math skit. Discuss the addition or subtraction that was shown. Write an equation on the board that represents the math that students were acting out, and have each group tell "how many" are at the conclusion of their skit.

ADDITION EQUATIONS

Directions: Write numbers in the equations. Draw objects under each number.

1)	2)
_____ + _____ = _____	_____ + _____ = _____
3)	4)
_____ + _____ = _____	_____ + _____ = _____
5)	6)
_____ + _____ = _____	_____ + _____ = _____
7)	8)
_____ + _____ = _____	_____ + _____ = _____
9)	10)
_____ + _____ = _____	_____ + _____ = _____

SUBTRACTION EQUATIONS

Directions: Write numbers in the equations. Draw objects below each equation. Cross out the number of objects being subtracted.

1) _____ – _____ = _____	2) _____ – _____ = _____
3) _____ – _____ = _____	4) _____ – _____ = _____
5) _____ – _____ = _____	6) _____ – _____ = _____
7) _____ – _____ = _____	8) _____ – _____ = _____
9) _____ – _____ = _____	10) _____ – _____ = _____

_____ fish swimming in a river. _____ fish join them.

_____ bunnies hopping. _____ bunnies join them.

_____ birds flying. _____ birds land on a rooftop.

_____ ducks paddling on a pond. _____ ducks fly away.

_____ kittens are playing. _____ more kittens come to play.

_____ squirrels sitting on a fence. _____ squirrels leave.

Operations and Algebraic Thinking: K.OA.2

"Understand addition as putting together and adding to, and understand subtraction as taking apart and taking from."

> 2. "Solve addition and subtraction word problems, and add and subtract within 10, e.g., by using objects or drawings to represent the problem."

BACKGROUND

To solve word problems, students must utilize skills in both reading and math. If students do not possess the required skills, they will find working with word problems to be frustrating, an experience that may lead to negative feelings about math. Possessing prerequisite skills is essential.

ACTIVITY: ADDITION AND SUBTRACTION WORD PROBLEMS

Students are to solve six word problems. They are to use counters and drawings to represent the problems.

MATERIALS

10 counters; crayons; reproducible, "Word Problems with Adding and Subtracting," for each student.

PROCEDURE

1. Hand out the materials. Explain that the reproducible contains six word problems that students are to solve. You might find it helpful to your students if you read the problems with them.

2. Instruct your students to do the following when solving the problems:

   - Read the problem carefully.
   - Ask what the problem is asking you to find.
   - Decide whether you must add or subtract.
   - Use counters to represent the problem.
   - Solve the problem.
   - Double-check your work.

3. Explain that students should use their counters to help them solve each problem. For example, to represent $5 + 2$, students should count out 5 counters, then count out 2 more. Combining the counters results in the sum, which is 7. To represent $3 - 2$, students should count out 3 counters, and then take 2 counters away, leaving 1.

4. Explain that after students have used counters to represent a problem, they are to draw and color objects—small circles, squares, or other figures—under the problem on the reproducible to represent the problem and its solution. To represent addition, suggest that students draw objects that represent the two addends and then show the sum. To represent subtraction, suggest that students draw the total number of objects and then cross out the number of objects that represent the number that is subtracted, showing the difference.

CLOSURE

Go over the answers to the problems as a class. Read each problem with your students, and ask volunteers to explain how they represented it and what its solution was. Show the representations and solutions on the board.

ANSWERS

Drawings should represent the equations. **(1)** $4 - 1 = 3$ **(2)** $5 + 2 = 7$ **(3)** $6 - 2 = 4$ **(4)** $7 + 3 = 10$ **(5)** $4 + 2 = 6$ **(6)** $8 - 6 = 2$

WORD PROBLEMS WITH ADDING AND SUBTRACTING

Directions: Solve each problem. Create a drawing for each problem.

1. 4 kittens were sleeping. 1 kitten woke up and walked away. How many kittens were still sleeping?

2. 5 deer were in the yard. 2 more deer came. How many deer were there in all?

3. 6 cookies were on a plate. Maria ate 2 cookies. How many cookies were left?

4. 7 goldfish were in a fish tank. Joe put 3 more goldfish in the tank. How many goldfish were in the tank?

5. It snowed 4 inches yesterday. It snowed 2 inches today. How much did it snow in all?

6. There were 8 pieces of pie. The family ate 6 pieces. How many pieces were left?

Operations and Algebraic Thinking: K.OA.3

"Understand addition as putting together and adding to, and understand subtraction as taking apart and taking from."

> 3. "Decompose numbers less than or equal to 10 into pairs in more than one way, e.g., by using objects or drawings, and record each decomposition by a drawing or equation."

BACKGROUND

Decomposing numbers into pairs helps students to understand that numbers can be broken down into other numbers. Conversely, students learn that two numbers can be combined to make another number.

ACTIVITY 1: GETTING TO 11

The teacher reads the book *12 Ways to Get to 11* by Eve Merriam to the class, highlighting and discussing math facts and concepts as she reads. (Note: Although this Standard requires students to decompose numbers less than or equal to 10, this book which includes the number 11 offers excellent examples of how numbers make up other numbers.)

MATERIALS

12 Ways to Get to 11 by Eve Merriam (Aladdin, 1996).

PROCEDURE

1. Have your students sit near you in a semi-circle so that you may share the illustrations as you read the book to them. Explain that you are going to read a book about different things that add up to 11.

2. As you read, pause often, show the pictures, and point out the objects that appear on the pages to get to 11.

3. Explain that 11 can be made from many different numbers. Expand this idea to include other numbers. For example, 4 can be made from $4 + 0, 0 + 4, 3 + 1, 1 + 3$, and $2 + 2$. Ask your students what numbers can make up other numbers. For example, what can 3 be made from? ($3 + 0, 0 + 3, 2 + 1$, and $1 + 2$) What can 5 be made from? ($5 + 0, 0 + 5, 4 + 1, 1 + 4, 3 + 2$, and $2 + 3$)

Discuss the story with your students. Review some of the ways to get to 11, as well as ways to get to the numbers from 2 to 10.

ACTIVITY 2: DECOMPOSING NUMBERS

Working in pairs or groups of three, students will use counters to decompose the numbers from 1 to 10. They will then represent the decompositions by drawings and equations. (Note: You may prefer to present this activity over two or three sessions.)

MATERIALS

10 counters; crayons for each student; 1 large sheet of drawing paper for each pair or group of students.

PROCEDURE

1. Hand out the materials and explain that numbers can be decomposed—broken down—into other numbers. For example, 3 can be decomposed into $3 + 0, 0 + 3, 2 + 1$, and $1 + 2$ because $3 = 3 + 0; 3 = 0 + 3; 3 = 2 + 1;$ and $3 = 1 + 2$.

2. Explain that students are to break the numbers 1 to 10 into at least two pairs of numbers. Students are to decompose each number, using their counters to represent the decomposition. Use 3 as an example again. Students can use their counters to represent $3 + 0, 0 + 3, 2 + 1,$ and $1 + 2$.

3. After students have decomposed a number using counters, they are to write the number on their paper, then write an equation and make a drawing that show the decomposition. Remind them that they are to decompose each of the numbers from 2 to 10 with at least two pairs of numbers. Provide 3 as an example for how their equations and drawings might look. Of course, they may use other objects in their drawings.

$$3 = 3 + 0 \quad \blacktriangle\blacktriangle\blacktriangle = \blacktriangle\blacktriangle\blacktriangle + 0 \qquad 3 = 2 + 1 \quad \blacktriangle\blacktriangle\blacktriangle = \blacktriangle\blacktriangle + \blacktriangle$$

Mention that 3 is now done for them. Note that there are other ways to decompose 3: $0 + 3$ and $1 + 2$. While for this activity students are only required to decompose each number into two pairs of numbers, you may encourage them to provide more pairs.

CLOSURE

Check your students' work. Discuss the decompositions they found. It is likely, especially with the larger numbers, that students decomposed numbers in various ways.

Note that the drawings should represent the numbers in each equation. The equations are provided in one form. For example, although 1 can be decomposed into $1 + 0$ and $0 + 1$, only one of the equations is shown. **(1)** $1 = 1 + 0$ **(2)** $2 = 2 + 0; 2 = 1 + 1$ **(3)** $3 = 3 + 0; 3 = 2 + 1$ **(4)** $4 = 4 + 0; 4 = 3 + 1; 4 = 2 + 2$ **(5)** $5 = 5 + 0; 5 = 4 + 1; 5 = 3 + 2$ **(6)** $6 = 6 + 0;$ $6 = 5 + 1; 6 = 4 + 2; 6 = 3 + 3$ **(7)** $7 = 7 + 0; 7 = 6 + 1; 7 = 5 + 2; 7 = 4 + 3$ **(8)** $8 = 8 + 0;$ $8 = 7 + 1; 8 = 6 + 2; 8 = 5 + 3; 8 = 4 + 4$ **(9)** $9 = 9 + 0; 9 = 8 + 1; 9 = 7 + 2; 9 = 6 + 3;$ $9 = 5 + 4$ **(10)** $10 = 10 + 0; 10 = 9 + 1; 10 = 8 + 2; 10 = 7 + 3; 10 = 6 + 4; 10 = 5 + 5$

Operations and Algebraic Thinking: K.OA.4

"Understand addition as putting together and adding to, and understand subtraction as taking apart and taking from."

> 4. "For any number from 1 to 9, find the number that makes 10 when added to the given number, e.g., by using objects or drawings, and record the answer with a drawing or equation."

BACKGROUND

As children learn basic addition facts, their general understanding of numbers expands. They gain an important insight once they realize that numbers can be formed by adding other numbers.

ACTIVITY: MAKING 10

Using number cards and counters, students will combine the numbers from 1 to 9 to make 10. They will record their answers with drawings and equations.

MATERIALS

10 counters; scissors; glue stick; crayons; reproducibles, "Adding Numbers to Make 10" and "Numbers 1 to 9," for each student. Optional: Scissors or paper cutter for the teacher.

PREPARATION

By this point of the school year, you may feel that your students are capable of cutting out number cards by themselves. However, if you feel that they are not yet ready, you must cut out the numbers on reproducible "Numbers 1 to 9" for them, providing each student with his or her own set of numbers.

PROCEDURE

1. Distribute the materials. Explain that the reproducible "Adding Numbers to Make 10" contains nine equations. The reproducible "Numbers 1 to 9" contains number cards, 1 to 9. Students are to cut out the number cards.

2. Explain that students are to complete the equations on the reproducible "Adding Numbers to Make 10." They are to use their counters to find the missing number in each equation and then glue the correct number card in the space to complete the equation. Finally, they are to draw objects under the numbers in each equation to represent the addition.

3. You may find it helpful to your students if you do the first equation, $1 + \underline{\hspace{1cm}} = 10$, together. Ask what number should be glued in the blank space. By using 1 counter to represent 1, students can count out 9 more counters to make a total of 10. Students should then glue the 9 card in the blank to complete the equation. They are then to draw objects, such as large dots or small circles, under the numbers to represent the numbers in the equations. Note that 6 and 9 each have a line beneath them so that these number cards are not confused.

4. Explain that students are to complete the other equations in the same manner.

CLOSURE

Discuss your students' work as a class. Ask volunteers to share their equations with the class, which you can write on the board. You may wish to draw objects to represent the numbers to clarify the concepts.

ANSWERS

Objects should match the numbers in each problem. **(1)** 9 **(2)** 5 **(3)** 2 **(4)** 6 **(5)** 8 **(6)** 4 **(7)** 1 **(8)** 7 **(9)** 3

Name _____

ADDING NUMBERS TO MAKE 10

Directions: Glue the correct number card in each equation. Draw objects under each number that show the number.

1)

$1 \; + \; \rule{3cm}{0.4pt} \; = \; 10$

_____

2)

$5 \; + \; \rule{3cm}{0.4pt} \; = \; 10$

_____

3)

$8 \; + \; \rule{3cm}{0.4pt} \; = \; 10$

_____

4)

$4 \; + \; \rule{3cm}{0.4pt} \; = \; 10$

_____

5)

$2 \; + \; \rule{3cm}{0.4pt} \; = \; 10$

_____

6)

$6 \; + \; \rule{3cm}{0.4pt} \; = \; 10$

_____

7)

$9 \; + \; \rule{3cm}{0.4pt} \; = \; 10$

_____

8)

$3 \; + \; \rule{3cm}{0.4pt} \; = \; 10$

_____

9)

$7 \; + \; \rule{3cm}{0.4pt} \; = \; 10$

_____

Directions: Cut out each number card.

8	5	9
4	2	7
3	1	6

Operations and Algebraic Thinking: K.OA.5

"Understand addition as putting together and adding to, and understand subtraction as taking apart and taking from."

> 5. "Fluently add and subtract within 5."

BACKGROUND

Being able to fluently add and subtract within 5 sets the foundation for adding and subtracting larger numbers quickly and accurately. Students who are fluent in these math facts no longer need objects to represent numbers.

 ACTIVITY 1: PILES OF CARDS

Working in groups, students sort cards containing equations and place those that have the same sums and differences in the same pile.

MATERIALS

Scissors; 6 small index cards (or small pieces of paper); reproducibles, "Addition and Subtraction Cards, I" and "Addition and Subtraction Cards, II," for each group of students. Optional: Scissors or paper cutter for the teacher.

PREPARATION

If you feel that your students are not yet ready to cut out cards from reproducibles, you must cut out the cards on reproducible "Addition and Subtraction Cards, I" and "Addition and Subtraction Cards, II." Combine the cards so that each group receives a total of 42 cards.

PROCEDURE

1. Hand out the materials. Instruct each group to write the numbers 0 to 5, one number on each index card. The cards represent the answers to the problems they must solve. They should place the index cards in order across a desk or table, leaving a little space between each one. Explain that each reproducible contains 21 cards that have addition and subtraction problems, one problem per card. Students are to cut out all 42 cards.

2. Explain that students are to solve the addition and subtraction problems. They are then to place each problem card by the index card whose number is the same as the card's

answer. For example, if the answer to a problem is 2, students would place that card by the index card with the number 2 on it. After students have solved all of the problems, they should double-check the piles to make certain that all of the answers in each pile are the same.

CLOSURE

Go over students' answers as a class. Ask for volunteers to say what cards they have in a pile. How many cards are in each pile? Students should correct the cards in their piles, if necessary.

ANSWERS

Answers	Sums and Differences
5	$0 + 5; 5 + 0; 1 + 4; 4 + 1; 2 + 3; 3 + 2; 5 - 0$
4	$0 + 4; 4 + 0; 1 + 3; 3 + 1; 2 + 2; 5 - 1; 4 - 0$
3	$0 + 3; 3 + 0; 1 + 2; 2 + 1; 5 - 2; 4 - 1; 3 - 0$
2	$0 + 2; 2 + 0; 1 + 1; 5 - 3; 4 - 2; 3 - 1; 2 - 0$
1	$0 + 1; 1 + 0; 5 - 4; 4 - 3; 3 - 2; 2 - 1; 1 - 0$
0	$0 + 0; 5 - 5; 4 - 4; 3 - 3; 2 - 2; 1 - 1; 0 - 0$

ACTIVITY 2: COLORING SUMS AND DIFFERENCES

Students will solve addition and subtraction problems contained in shapes. They will color the shapes according to the answers to the problems.

MATERIALS

Red, blue, green, yellow, and orange crayons; reproducible, "Coloring Addition and Subtraction Problems," for each student.

PROCEDURE

1. Distribute the materials. Explain that the reproducible contains addition and subtraction problems that students are to solve. The problems appear in triangles. Students are to color all the triangles that have the same answer with the same color. At the bottom of the sheet is a color code, showing how the triangles should be colored. Triangles that contain

problems with the answer of 5 are to be colored red, triangles that contain problems with the answer of 4 should be colored blue, and so on.

2. To make sure that your students understand what colors they are to use, tell them to place a red mark under 5, a blue mark under 4, a green mark under 3, a yellow mark under 2, and an orange mark under 1.

3. Instruct your students to solve the problems and write the answer to each problem in the same triangle as the problem. They should then color the triangles.

CLOSURE

Check your students' work and discuss problems they found confusing.

ANSWERS

The correct colors for the triangles are shown below.

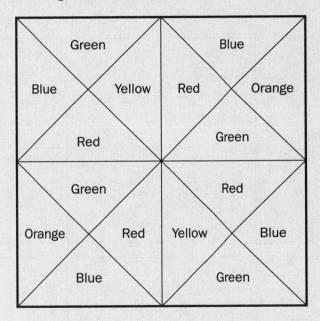

$0 + 5$	$5 - 1$	$0 + 1$
$5 - 2$	$1 + 2$	$1 + 4$
$5 - 4$	$4 - 1$	$3 - 0$
$3 + 0$	$2 + 3$	$2 + 0$
$5 - 5$	$2 + 2$	$4 - 2$
$1 + 0$	$4 - 3$	$4 + 0$
$3 + 1$	$4 - 4$	$1 - 0$

2 − 0	0 + 4	0 + 0
1 + 1	1 + 3	3 − 1
3 − 3	2 − 2	3 + 2
4 + 1	0 + 3	5 − 0
1 − 1	0 − 0	3 − 2
2 + 1	5 − 3	2 − 1
4 − 0	0 + 2	5 + 0

Name_____

COLORING ADDITION AND SUBTRACTION PROBLEMS

Directions: Solve each problem. Color the space the problem is in. Use the color code below.

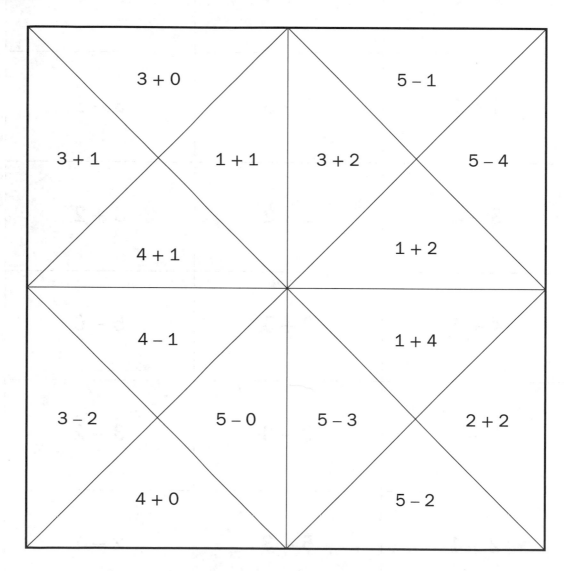

Color the spaces of problems with the answers of:

5 – red   4 – blue   3 – green

2 – yellow   1 – orange

Number and Operations in Base Ten: K.NBT.1

"Work with numbers 11–19 to gain foundations for place value."

1. "Compose and decompose numbers from 11 to 19 into ten ones and some further ones, e.g., by using objects or drawings, and record each composition or decomposition by a drawing or equation (e.g., $18 = 10 + 8$); understand that these numbers are composed of ten ones and one, two, three, four, five, six, seven, eight, or nine ones."

BACKGROUND

Our number system is a base-10 system. One-digit numbers denote ones. 10 means a group of 10 ones with no further ones. 11 means 1 ten and 1 one; 12 means 1 ten and 2 ones, and so on. This pattern continues to 19, which is 1 ten and 9 ones. Understanding the basics of our number system is fundamental to understanding numbers greater than 10.

ACTIVITY: TENS AND ONES

Students will use counters to compose the numbers 11 to 19. They will then decompose the numbers with drawings and by writing equations. (Note: You might prefer to present this activity in two or three sessions.)

MATERIALS

19 counters; crayons; reproducibles, "Numbers: Tens and Ones, I," "Numbers: Tens and Ones, II," and "Numbers: Tens and Ones, III," for each student.

PROCEDURE

1. Hand out the materials. Explain that the reproducibles contain frames for the numbers 11 to 19. The numbers are not in order. (If you decide to present the activity in three sessions, hand out only the first reproducible on the first day, the second reproducible on the second, and the third reproducible on the third.)

2. Explain that students are to use their counters to compose the numbers 11 to 19 as they are presented on the reproducibles. They are to then color in the correct number of frames to show the number as a ten and some further ones. Finally, they are to write an equation that shows the decomposition of the number into 10 ones and additional ones.

3. For an example, do the number 11 on the first reproducible as a class.

- Instruct your students to use their counters to represent the number 11, first by counting out 10 counters. Ask: How many more counters will you need to make 11? Students should realize that they will need 1 more counter. Explain that 10 ones and 1 one make 11. This is the same as 1 ten and 1 one.

- Next tell your students to color 10 frames to represent 10 ones (or 1 ten), and then 1 more frame to represent 1 more.

- After they have colored the frames representing 11, ask: What equation can you write to show the frames that you colored? The equation is $11 = 10 + 1$. Instruct students to write the equation on the line under the frames.

- Explain that students are to follow this procedure for the other numbers.

CLOSURE

Check your students' work. Discuss how each of the numbers 11 to 19 is composed of one ten and a specific number of ones. Also, remind your students that each number can be decomposed into tens and ones. Ask for volunteers to share some equations showing decompositions, for example, $16 = 10 + 6$.

ANSWERS

The colored frames for each number should match the following equations.
$11 = 10 + 1; 14 = 10 + 4; 17 = 10 + 7; 15 = 10 + 5; 18 = 10 + 8; 12 = 10 + 2; 13 = 10 + 3; 19 = 10 + 9; 16 = 10 + 6$

Name _____

NUMBERS: TENS AND ONES, I

Directions: Color the frames to show each number. Write an equation to show the frames you colored.

11

_____

14

_____

17

_____

NUMBERS: TENS AND ONES, II

Directions: Color the frames to show each number. Write an equation to show the frames you colored.

15

_____

18

_____

12

_____

NUMBERS: TENS AND ONES, III

Directions: Color the frames to show each number. Write an equation to show the frames you colored.

13

19

16

Measurement and Data: K.MD.1

"Describe and compare measurable attributes."

1. "Describe measurable attributes of objects, such as length or weight. Describe several measurable attributes of a single object."

BACKGROUND

Objects may be described by their measurable attributes. Common measurable attributes include length, width, height, and weight. Developing an intuitive sense of size is a prerequisite skill for conducting actual measurement.

 ### ACTIVITY: DRAW, SHOW, AND TELL

For this activity, students will first work individually and then in groups. Working individually, students will draw pictures of objects of their choice. In groups they will discuss the attributes of the pictures they drew. Groups will share their drawings and the attributes they found with the class.

MATERIALS

Crayons; drawing paper for each student.

PROCEDURE

1. Explain to your students that objects have measurable attributes. An object may be described by how long it is, how wide it is, how high it is, or how much it weighs. For example, a telephone pole might be described as being high or long. A big truck might be described as being very heavy. Your classroom might be long and wide. Its ceiling might be high. Ask your students to offer examples of other things and describe their measurable attributes. Emphasize that most objects have several measurable attributes.

2. Hand out the materials. Explain that students are to choose something they would like to draw. For example, they might decide to draw a house, an airplane, a boat, a car, a truck, a skyscraper, a desk, a book, a pencil—their possible choices are limited only by their imaginations. Ask your students to name other possible objects to draw. This will help those students who might be having trouble finding an idea for drawing.

3. Explain that after they have drawn and colored their picture, students are to work in their group. They are to discuss the measurable attributes of the things they have

drawn, including length, width, height, and weight. For example, a student might say, "The building I drew is very high and very wide."

4. As your students are working, visit with the various groups to provide guidance and answer any questions they might have about measurable attributes.

CLOSURE

Have your students sit in a circle as a class. Ask for volunteers to hold up their drawings and explain the object they drew, including its measurable attributes. Be sure to point out any attributes students might have overlooked.

Measurement and Data: K.MD.2

"Describe and compare measurable attributes."

> 2. "Directly compare two objects with a measurable attribute in common, to see which object has 'more of'/'less of' the attribute, and describe the difference."

BACKGROUND

Once students can identify common measurable attributes of objects and are able to compare attributes, they can determine differences between objects. For example, a side of one object might have "more" length than a side of another object. In such a case, one side is longer than the other. Conversely, if a side of one object has "less" length than a side of another object, one side may be described as being shorter than the other.

 ## ACTIVITY: COMPARING ATTRIBUTES OF OBJECTS

Working in pairs or groups of three, students will directly compare a measurable attribute in pairs of objects. They will describe the differences and share their results with the class.

MATERIALS

Various items in the classroom, including typical materials such as pencils, crayons, books, paper, as well as desks, tables, doors, windows, and so on.

PROCEDURE

1. Explain that measurable attributes of objects include such things as length, width, height, and weight. These attributes can be compared and the differences between them can be easily seen. Provide some examples. One bookshelf might have more length than another; one room might be wider than another; one chair might be higher than another; one knapsack might weigh less than another.

2. Explain that students are to work with their partner or partners, and find objects that have measurable attributes in common. Ask your students to name some objects that have measurable attributes in common. Along with ideas they might offer, following are some you might suggest:

   - The length of a pencil to the length of a crayon

   - The length of a student's arm to the length of her index finger

- The width of a large sheet of construction paper to the width of a small sheet of construction paper

- The width of the screen of a large TV to the width of a computer screen

- The height of the door to the height of a teacher

- The heights of different plants around the room

- The weight of a dictionary to the weight of a small paperback

- The weight of a sheet of paper to the weight of a ream of paper

3. Explain that partners or group members are to discuss and compare measurable attributes of at least one pair of objects. They may choose the objects that they wish to compare and describe the attributes in terms of one being longer, shorter, higher, wider, heavier, or lighter than the other, or one having more of or less of an attribute than the other.

CLOSURE

Have each pair or group of students report to the class the objects and measurable attributes they compared. Discuss the attributes and point out any attributes that students did not mention.

Measurement and Data: K.MD.3

"Classify objects and count the number of objects in each category."

> 3. "Classify objects into given categories; count the numbers of objects in each category and sort the categories by count."

BACKGROUND

Sorting, classifying, and counting objects are basic skills that most of us use every day. Sorting the laundry; making sure there is enough food, plates, and utensils for the annual family picnic; and packing luggage for vacation are just some tasks that are dependent on the ability to sort, classify, and count objects. For young children, acquiring such skills is an important achievement.

 ACTIVITY: SORTING, CLASSIFYING, AND COUNTING OBJECTS

Working in pairs or groups of three, students will be given a container filled with various objects. The number and types of objects will vary by pair or group. Students will sort, classify, and count the objects and then record their findings with drawings and numbers.

MATERIALS

Three different kinds of objects (6 to 10 of each item), such as counters, beads, buttons, paper clips, and so on; a small plastic cup (or similar container) for each pair or group of students; crayons; drawing paper for each student.

PREPARATION

Place the three kinds of objects into plastic cups, one cup for each pair or group of students. The number of each kind of objects should vary between 6 and 10. For example, one cup may contain 7 counters, 9 beads, and 10 buttons; another cup may contain 6 counters, 10 beads, and 8 buttons.

PROCEDURE

1. Hand out the materials. Explain that the cup each pair or group of students received contains three different kinds of objects. The number of each kind of object is different.

2. Explain that students are to empty their cups. They are to sort and classify the objects into separate groups. They are then to count the number of items of each group.

3. Explain that after students have sorted, classified, and counted the objects, they are to record their findings by drawing an example of the objects in each group and writing the number of the objects. Although students worked together in sorting, classifying, and counting, each student is to make his or her own drawing.

CLOSURE

Discuss your students' results. Ask pairs or groups of students what kinds of objects they sorted, and how many objects of each kind they counted. Display your students' drawings.

Geometry: K.G.1

"Identify and describe shapes (squares, circles, triangles, rectangles, hexagons, cubes, cones, cylinders, and spheres)."

> 1. "Describe objects in the environment using names of shapes, and describe the relative positions of these objects using terms such as *above, below, beside, in front of, behind,* and *next to.*"

BACKGROUND

Geometric shapes are found everywhere. Identifying the shapes of objects and describing their relative positions to other objects helps to develop students' awareness of the relationships of objects around them.

ACTIVITY: FINDING SHAPES

Working in groups, students will identify geometric shapes in the classroom and place sticky notes on selected objects. Groups will share the objects they selected with the class by naming them and describing the relative positions of the objects.

MATERIALS

5 sticky notes for each group of students (a different color for each group); poster paper; ruler; markers for the teacher. (Note: If you do not have different colors of sticky notes, you may simply label the notes with numbers—Group 1, Group 2, and so on.)

PREPARATION

Create a poster of geometric shapes, showing the word names and examples. The poster should show a square, circle, triangle, rectangle, hexagon, cube, cone, cylinder, and sphere. Display the poster in the classroom for your students. (Note: Keep this poster for use with following Standards and activities.)

PROCEDURE

1. Review the shapes and their names on the poster you made. Encourage students to refer to the poster if they are not sure of a shape or its name. Also discuss the terms *above, on top of, under, below, beside, in front of, behind,* and *next to,* providing examples that show how they may be used to describe an object's relative position.

2. Hand out the sticky notes. Explain that each group has 5 sticky notes and that each group's sticky notes are a different color. For example, group 1 might have red notes, group 2 might have blue notes, and so on.

3. Explain that each group is to go around the classroom and find examples of shapes that are displayed on the poster you made. When they find one of the shapes, they are to place a sticky note on the shape. For example, the surface of a table may be a rectangle, a bulletin board may be a square, a globe is a sphere, and a marker is a cylinder. Note that each group of students has only 5 sticky notes and will not be able to label each shape on the poster. They should, however, label 5 different shapes.

4. Tell your students to look closely at the many different objects in the classroom, because sometimes the shapes they are looking for are "hidden" in plain sight. The long, narrow legs of a chair, for instance, might be cylinders.

5. Explain that students should be prepared to share their results with the class. They should be able to describe the relative position of each shape by using the terms *above, on top of, below, under, in front of, behind, beside,* and *next to.* For example, the globe (a sphere) is on top of the table (a rectangle).

CLOSURE

One at a time have each group go to their sticky notes, identify the shape, and describe its relative position in regard to other objects.

Geometry: K.G.2

"Identify and describe shapes (squares, circles, triangles, rectangles, hexagons, cubes, cones, cylinders, and spheres)."

> 2. "Correctly name shapes regardless of their orientations or overall size."

BACKGROUND

Even though they may know the names of shapes, students may be unable to recognize the shapes if the shapes are presented in a different position or size. For example, they may not recognize a square if it is tipped on its side. Similarly, students might not recognize a triangle if it has a large obtuse angle and long sides. Being able to recognize shapes, regardless of orientation, is a sign that students have mastered this concept.

ACTIVITY 1: IDENTIFYING AND MATCHING

Students will be given a reproducible with various geometric shapes. They will cut the shapes out, identify them, and glue them under their correct name.

MATERIALS

Scissors; glue stick; 1 sheet of large construction paper; reproducibles, "Names and Shapes, I" and "Names and Shapes, II," for each student. Optional: Document camera; computer; digital projector; transparencies; overhead projector for the teacher.

PREPARATION

Display the poster that you made for the activity for Standard K.G.1.

PROCEDURE

1. Review the names and examples of squares, circles, triangles, rectangles, hexagons, cubes, cones, cylinders, and spheres.

2. Explain that all of these shapes can come in different sizes. Different kinds of triangles may appear to be different shapes entirely because of the degrees of their angles, but they are still triangles. Shapes may also be positioned differently. This is called a shape's orientation.

3. Provide an example of a square with two sizes and two orientations, such as the example below.

4. Explain that both shapes are squares. The one on the left is smaller than the one on the right, which is turned (rotated). Ask your students to imagine turning the square on the right so that it has the same orientation as the square on the left. (You may find it helpful to use a document camera or an overhead projector, and rotate squares to show different orientations.) It will now be easier for students to see that both shapes are squares. Provide some other examples, such as an obtuse triangle and an acute triangle as shown below. Explain that although they may appear to be different, the shapes are triangles. Each has three corners (vertices) and three sides.

5. Hand out the materials. Explain that students are to cut out the names of the shapes and the shapes on the reproducibles.

6. Explain that they should place their construction paper lengthwise on their desk or table, and then place the names of the shapes across the top, leaving some space between each name. After spacing out the names of the shapes, they are to glue the names to the paper. Your students will no doubt find it helpful if you demonstrate this.

7. Explain that students are to now identify the shapes. Some of the shapes have different sizes and orientations, so students must look at them closely. Suggest that turning the shapes and changing their orientation may help students to recognize them. After they have identified a shape, students are to glue it under its name on their construction paper. There is at least one example of every shape, but there is more than one for some shapes.

CLOSURE

Check your students' work. Ask for volunteers to report how many examples of a shape they found. Point out the different sizes and orientations of the shapes. Ask students how they were able to identify the shapes.

The number of shapes is provided for each name. Squares, 3; Circles, 2; Triangles, 3; Rectangles, 2; Hexagons, 1; Cubes, 1; Cones, 1; Cylinders, 1. Spheres: 1

 ACTIVITY 2: A VIRTUAL GEOBOARD

Using a virtual geoboard at a Web site, the teacher will project various geometric shapes of different sizes and orientations. Students are to name the shapes.

MATERIALS

Computer with Internet access; digital projector for the teacher.

PROCEDURE

1. Explain that shapes come in different sizes and orientations. Review the names and examples of shapes, including squares, rectangles, triangles, and hexagons. (Note: You will not be able to make circles, cubes, cones, cylinders, or spheres on the virtual geoboard because they are either curved lines or three-dimensional shapes.)

2. Go to http://nlvm.usu.edu/. Click on "Pre-K–2," "Measurement," and then click on "Geoboard." Explain to students that you are going to make some shapes, and that students are to name the shapes. The shapes will be in different sizes and orientations.

3. To create a shape, click on a virtual rubber band under "Bands," and drag the band to the board. Place it on a peg on the board. By clicking on the band again, you can stretch it to another peg. By clicking on it once more, you can stretch it to make a triangle. You can use the bands to make squares, rectangles, triangles, and hexagons of various sizes and orientations. You can make several figures on the same screen. To delete a specific figure, highlight it by clicking on a line of the figure and click on "Delete." To clear all figures from the screen, click on "Clear." To color a figure, highlight it and then click on a color.

4. Create several shapes of different sizes and orientations and ask your students to name the shapes.

CLOSURE

Review the shapes. Place one example of each on the geoboard at the same time: a square, a rectangle, a triangle, and a hexagon. Ask students to name each one.

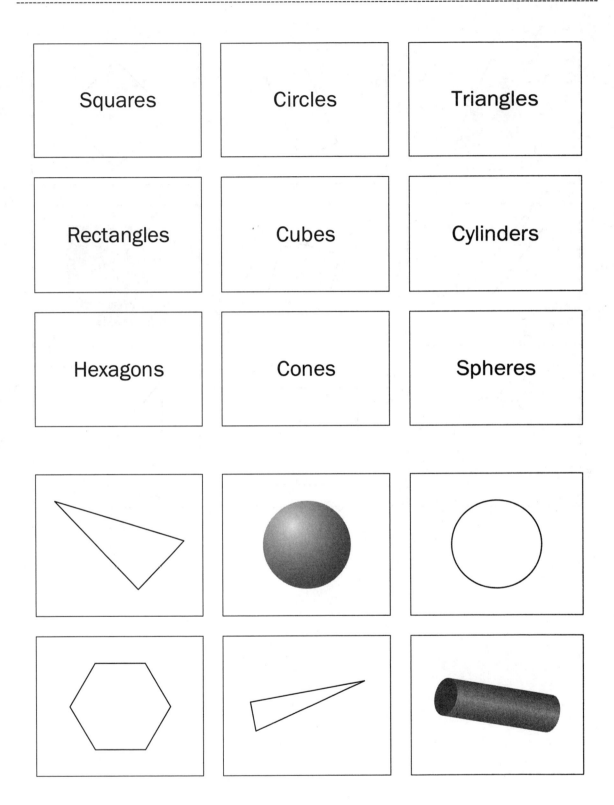

Squares	Circles	Triangles
Rectangles	Cubes	Cylinders
Hexagons	Cones	Spheres

NAMES AND SHAPES, II

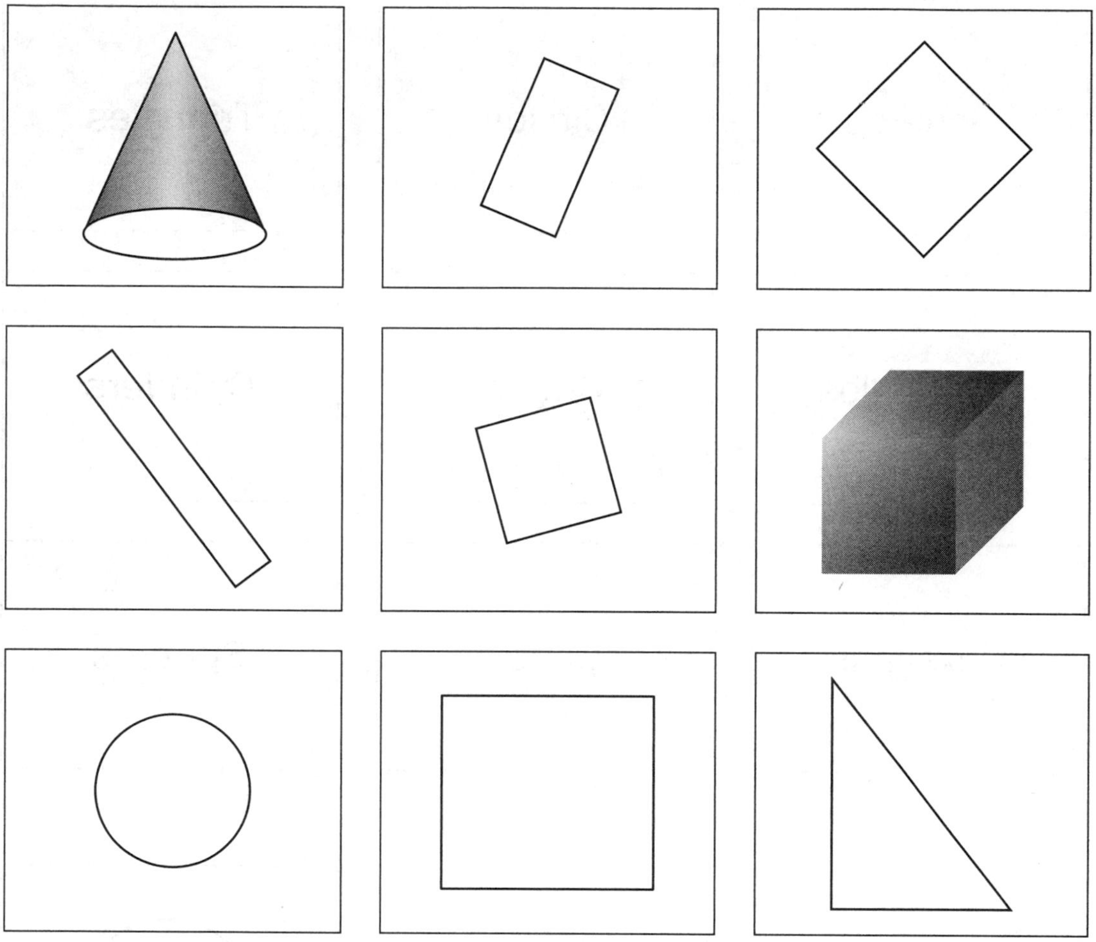

Geometry: K.G.3

"Identify and describe shapes (squares, circles, triangles, rectangles, hexagons, cubes, cones, cylinders, and spheres)."

> 3. "Identify shapes as two-dimensional (lying in a plane, 'flat') or three-dimensional ('solid')."

BACKGROUND

We live in a three-dimensional world where shapes have length, width, and height. Because they have three dimensions, these shapes are often described as being solid. Examples include dice (cubes) and a can of soup (cylinder). Flat shapes have two-dimensions: length and width. Examples include the side of a box (rectangle) or the top of a cylinder (circle). Recognizing the difference between two- and three-dimensional shapes lays the foundation for working with plane and solid figures in later grades.

ACTIVITY: FLAT OR SOLID

Working in groups of three or four, students play a game in which they pick cards that show pictures of two-dimensional or three-dimensional shapes. Students are to decide whether the shapes on the cards are flat or solid. Students receive one point for each correct answer, and the student with the most points at the end of the game wins.

MATERIALS

Scissors; reproducibles, "Flat or Solid Picture Cards, I" and "Flat or Solid Picture Cards, II," for each group of students; reproducible, "Flat or Solid Score Sheet," one full page for every two students. Optional: Scissors or paper cutter for the teacher.

PREPARATION

Make enough copies of the reproducible "Flat or Solid Score Sheet" so that each student has his or her own score sheet. Cut out the individual score sheets. (Note: Depending on your students, you may prefer to cut out the picture cards as well.)

PROCEDURE

1. Hand out the materials. Explain that students will play a game called "Flat or Solid." Each group has two reproducibles that contain picture cards. The picture cards are numbered. Each student has a score sheet. Instruct students to write their name on their score sheet.

2. Explain that students are to cut out the picture cards and place them face down in a pile. The cards do not have to be in order.

3. Explain the rules of the game. Students will take turns picking cards. The first student picks a card and presents the card to the other students in the group. All members of the group individually decide whether the shape on the card is flat or solid. Then, on their score sheet, they find the number of the card and circle whether the shape is flat or solid. The next student picks a card and the same procedure continues. Caution students to make sure that they circle their answers according to a card's number.

4. Explain that the game ends after all of the cards have been picked. For every correct answer, a student receives 1 point. The student with the most points in the group at the end of the game wins.

CLOSURE

Starting with number 1, announce whether the cards contain a picture that represents a flat or solid shape. Have students correct their answers and then count the number of answers they got correct. Ask: Who had the most points in each group? Who had the most points in the class? Discuss any shapes that students had trouble identifying as being flat or solid.

ANSWERS

(1) Solid (2) Flat (3) Solid (4) Flat (5) Flat (6) Flat (7) Solid (8) Flat (9) Solid (10) Solid (11) Flat (12) Solid (13) Flat (14) Flat (15) Flat (16) Solid (17) Solid (18) Flat

1.
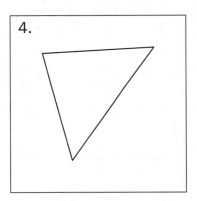

2.
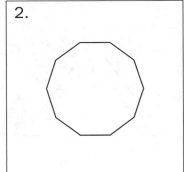

3.
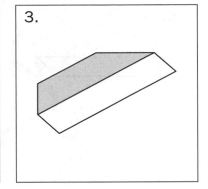

4.
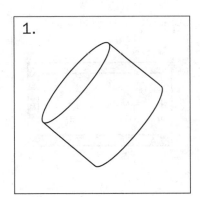

5.
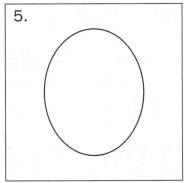

6.
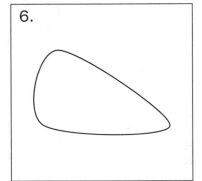

7.
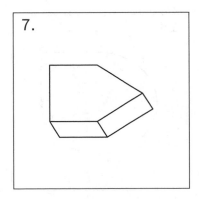

8.
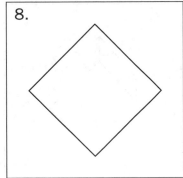

9.
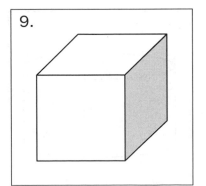

10.

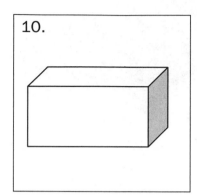

11.

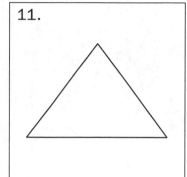

12.

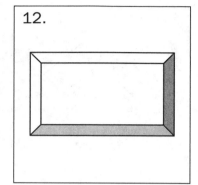

13.

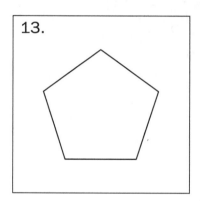

14.

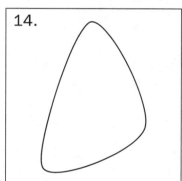

15.

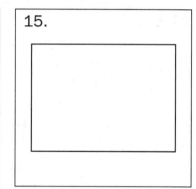

16.

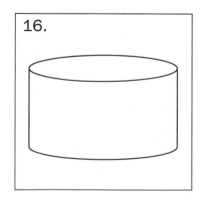

17.

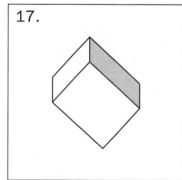

18.

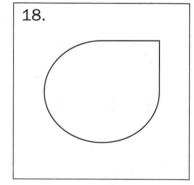

FLAT OR SOLID SCORE SHEET

Name _____

   1) Flat or Solid   2) Flat or Solid   3) Flat or Solid

   4) Flat or Solid   5) Flat or Solid   6) Flat or Solid

   7) Flat or Solid   8) Flat or Solid   9) Flat or Solid

10) Flat or Solid   11) Flat or Solid   12) Flat or Solid

13) Flat or Solid   14) Flat or Solid   15) Flat or Solid

16) Flat or Solid   17) Flat or Solid   18) Flat or Solid

- -

FLAT OR SOLID SCORE SHEET

Name _____

   1) Flat or Solid   2) Flat or Solid   3) Flat or Solid

   4) Flat or Solid   5) Flat or Solid   6) Flat or Solid

   7) Flat or Solid   8) Flat or Solid   9) Flat or Solid

10) Flat or Solid   11) Flat or Solid   12) Flat or Solid

13) Flat or Solid   14) Flat or Solid   15) Flat or Solid

16) Flat or Solid   17) Flat or Solid   18) Flat or Solid

Geometry: K.G.4

"Analyze, compare, create, and compose shapes."

4. "Analyze and compare two- and three-dimensional shapes, in different sizes and orientations, using informal language to describe their similarities, differences, parts (e.g., number of sides and vertices/'corners') and other attributes (e.g., having sides of equal lengths)."

BACKGROUND

In order to analyze and compare two- and three-dimensional shapes, students must be able to recognize the shapes and their attributes. Being familiar with the similarities, differences, and parts of shapes enables students to make accurate comparisons between them. Following are descriptions of common shapes:

- A square has four sides of equal length and four right angles. (You might want to mention that right angles are like the corners of a standard sheet of paper.)
- A rectangle has four right angles and four sides. Opposite sides have the same length.
- A triangle has three sides and three vertices (corners).
- A pentagon has five sides and five vertices (corners).
- A hexagon has six sides and six vertices (corners).
- A circle is round. It has no sides or vertices (corners).
- A cube is a solid figure that has six square faces.
- A cone is a solid figure that has a flat round base and a point (vertex).
- A cylinder is a solid (or hollow) object in the shape of a can.
- A sphere is a solid figure like a ball.

 ## ACTIVITY 1: ANALYZING AND COMPARING TWO-DIMENSIONAL SHAPES

Working individually first, students will identify two-dimensional shapes of different sizes and orientations by coloring the same types of shapes the same color. They will then work in a group to analyze and compare the shapes.

MATERIALS

Blue, red, green, orange, and yellow crayons; reproducibles, "Two-Dimensional Shapes" and "Describing Two-Dimensional Shapes," for each student.

PROCEDURE

1. Explain that two-dimensional shapes lie flat in a plane. Review examples of two-dimensional shapes, comprising squares, rectangles, triangles, circles, and hexagons. Note the descriptions of each shape, as provided in the Background.

2. Distribute the materials. Explain that the first reproducible, "Two-Dimensional Shapes," contains various two-dimensional shapes in different sizes and orientations. A color code for coloring the shapes is on the bottom of the sheet. The second reproducible, "Describing Two-Dimensional Shapes," contains guidelines that will help students to describe the shapes.

3. Explain that students are to first work individually and color the shapes according to the color code at the bottom of the reproducible. For example, squares should be colored blue, rectangles should be colored red, and so on.

4. Explain that after they have colored the shapes, they are to compare their work with the work of the other members of their group. Students are to check that all group members have colored the shapes correctly.

5. Next, instruct your students to work in their group and analyze and compare the shapes, and then complete the reproducible "Describing Two-Dimensional Shapes." (Depending on your students, you might find it helpful to work through this part of the activity as a class. You might read the information for each shape, one at a time, and then allow students to discuss the answers in their groups and complete the reproducible together as a group.)

CLOSURE

Discuss students' results. Ask for volunteers to describe each of the shapes in informal terms, as was provided in the Background.

ANSWERS

There are 3 squares, 3 rectangles, 4 triangles, 3 circles, and 2 hexagons.

ACTIVITY 2: VIRTUAL TWO-DIMENSIONAL SHAPES

Using a Web site, the teacher will lead an activity in which students must identify, analyze, and compare two-dimensional shapes.

MATERIALS

Computer with Internet access; digital projector for the teacher.

1. Explain that two-dimensional shapes may appear in different sizes, orientations, and colors. You will present various shapes on a Web site, and students must identify the shapes according to shape, size, and color.

2. Go to http://nlvm.usu.edu/. Click on "Pre-K–2," "Measurement," and then click on "Attribute Blocks." You will find an oval containing shapes with other shapes outside the oval. The shapes are squares, rectangles, triangles, circles, and pentagons.

3. Explain to your students that the shapes inside the oval have something in common. For example, they might all be triangles; they might all be big shapes; or they might all be the same color. Your students' task is to decide which shapes outside the oval should be moved to the inside. Clicking on a shape allows you to drag the shape inside the oval.

4. Ask for volunteers to suggest which shapes to move inside the oval, based on their shape, size, or color. Encourage students to refer to the shapes by name. Move the shapes your students suggest one at a time. To see if they are correct, click on "Check." If the "Try again" message appears, ask your students to reconsider what shapes should be placed in the oval. Clicking on "New Problem" provides a new set of shapes.

CLOSURE

Discuss the various shapes that were on the Web site. Ask students to informally describe a square, rectangle, triangle, pentagon, and circle.

 ACTIVITY 3: ANALYZING AND COMPARING THREE-DIMENSIONAL SHAPES

Working in groups, students will use interlocking centimeter cubes to create, analyze, and compare three-dimensional shapes. They will share their results with the members of their group and the class.

MATERIALS

16 interlocking cubes for each student.

PREPARATION

Use interlocking cubes to create an example of a three-dimensional shape to show to your students.

PROCEDURE

1. Review three-dimensional shapes. Emphasize that three-dimensional shapes have length, width, and height. They may be described as being solid as opposed to being flat. Show your students the shape you made and point out its dimensions.

2. Hand out the interlocking centimeter cubes.

3. Explain that each student is to use his or her cubes to create a three-dimensional shape. After they have made their shapes, students are to analyze and compare their shapes with the shapes made by the members of their group. They should describe the number of sides a shape has, the number of its vertices (corners), and the length of its sides compared to other shapes.

CLOSURE

Discuss students' results. Ask for volunteers to show and describe the shapes they created to the class. Ask your students if changing the orientation or position of a shape changes the shape in any way.

Name _____

TWO-DIMENSIONAL SHAPES

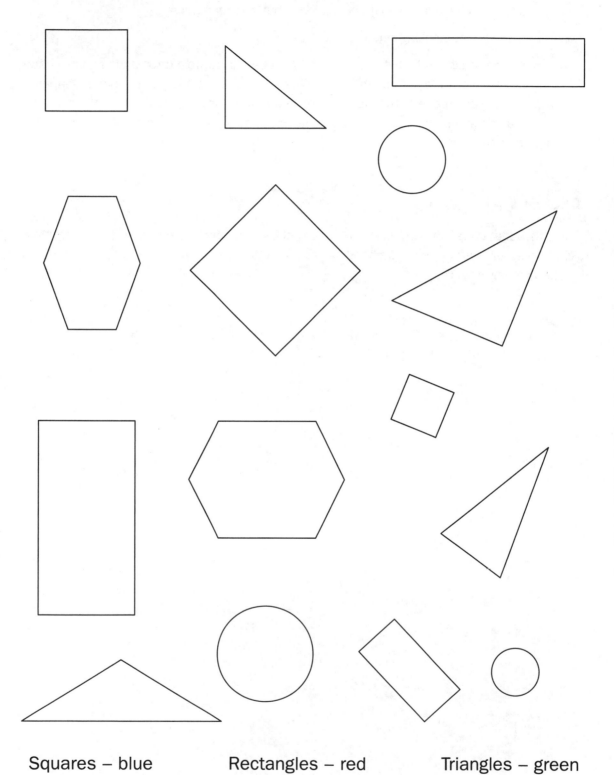

Squares – blue   Rectangles – red   Triangles – green

Hexagons – orange   Circles – yellow

Name _____

DESCRIBING TWO-DIMENSIONAL SHAPES

Fill in the blanks.

Square

Number of Sides _____   Number of Corners _____

Rectangle

Number of Sides _____   Number of Corners _____

Triangle

Number of Sides _____   Number of Corners _____

Hexagon

Number of Sides _____   Number of Corners _____

Circle

Number of Sides _____   Number of Corners _____

Which shape has sides of equal length? _____

Which shape has no sides or corners? _____

Geometry: K.G.5

"Analyze, compare, create, and compose shapes."

> 5. "Model shapes in the world by building shapes from components (e.g., sticks and clay balls) and drawing shapes."

BACKGROUND

Models provide visual representation of shapes. Creating models of shapes that occur in the real world helps students to understand how common shapes may be found just about everywhere.

ACTIVITY: MAKING MODELS

In this two-day activity, students will use clay to create models of shapes found in the real world. After they create their clay models, students will draw a picture of their model. They will then compare their model and drawing with the models and drawings of other students.

MATERIALS

4 to 6 ounces of modeling clay; drawing paper; rulers; crayons for each student; paper towels for cleanup.

PROCEDURE

Day One

1. Hand out the clay. Explain that students are to use their clay to create shapes that will model objects in the real world. Offer some examples, which you may sketch on the board, such as:

   • A house, using a triangle and a rectangle or square.

- A flagpole and a flag, using two rectangles.

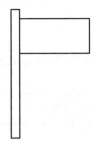

- A boat, using a triangle, a rectangle, and a square.

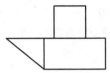

- A car, using circles and rectangles.

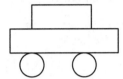

2. Brainstorm with your students to generate ideas for other shapes they can use for their models.

3. Encourage your students to be neat and accurate with their work, but also creative.

4. At the end of the period, collect students' models and store them for use on Day Two.

Day Two

1. Hand out the drawing paper, rulers, crayons, and the clay models students made previously.

2. Explain that students are to draw pictures of their models. Suggest that they color their pictures.

CLOSURE

Discuss how the models and drawings students made are alike and different. Ask your students: Which—the clay model or the drawing—is three-dimensional and which is two-dimensional? Have students share their models and drawings with a partner. Students should describe the shapes they used to make their models and drawings. Ask for volunteers to show and describe their work to the class.

Geometry: K.G.6

"Analyze, compare, create, and compose shapes."

> 6. "Compose simple shapes to form larger shapes."

BACKGROUND

Simple and complex geometric figures are found throughout the world. Simple shapes are often combined to make complex shapes. Recognizing how simple shapes combine to form complex shapes is an important skill that leads to the concept that a whole may be made up of many parts.

ACTIVITY: COMBINING SHAPES

Students will be given shapes that they will cut out and then combine to form more complex shapes.

MATERIALS

Scissors; glue stick; crayons; reproducibles, "Cut-Out Shapes, I" and "Cut-Out Shapes, II," for each student; transparent tape for the teacher.

PREPARATION

Use transparent tape to tape two $8\frac{1}{2}$-inch by 11-inch sheets of paper to form an $8\frac{1}{2}$-inch by 22-inch rectangle as a visual aid.

PROCEDURE

1. Explain that many shapes are often formed by combining simpler shapes. Show students the $8\frac{1}{2}$-inch by 22-inch rectangle you made. Explain that this rectangle was made by putting two smaller rectangles together. Point out the two pieces.

2. Hand out the materials. Explain that each reproducible has four rows of shapes, followed by a dotted line and a larger shape. Students are to cut out all of the shapes in a row, and then combine the smaller shapes to make the larger shape. Students should place the smaller shapes so that they fit onto the larger shape without any gaps or overlaps. Once students see that the shapes fit, they should glue the smaller shapes onto the larger shapes. They may color the shapes if they wish.

3. Caution your students to cut out and complete one row at a time to prevent the shapes from different rows getting mixed up.

Check your students' work. Discuss any shapes that are the same but may be in a different orientation.

ANSWERS

Possible combinations are shown below.

1.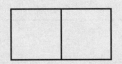

2.

3.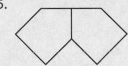

4.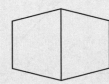

5.

6.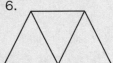

7.

8.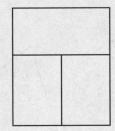

Cut These Out | Make These

1.

2.

3.

4.

Cut These Out   Make These

5.

6.

7.

8.

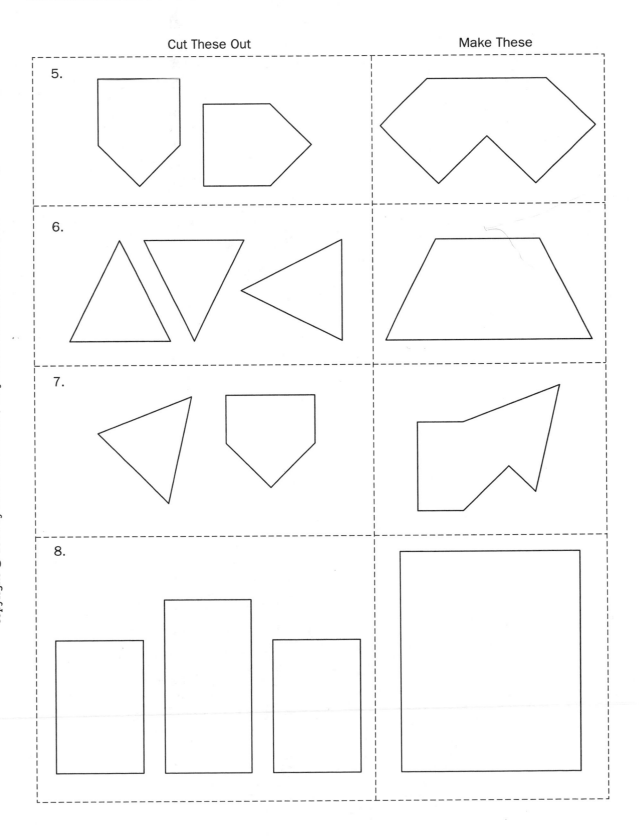

Standards and Activities for Grade 1

Operations and Algebraic Thinking: 1.OA.1

"Represent and solve problems involving addition and subtraction."

1. "Use addition and subtraction within 20 to solve word problems involving situations of adding to, taking from, putting together, taking apart, and comparing, with unknowns in all positions, e.g., by using objects, drawings, and equations with a symbol for the unknown number to represent the problem."

BACKGROUND

Representing addition and subtraction with word problems that involve various situations broadens children's understanding of problem solving. Objects and drawings can be used to model problems and help children visualize the numbers and processes that result in a solution. Writing equations with unknowns is a more abstract way to represent problems and find their solutions.

 ACTIVITY 1: WORD PROBLEMS—ADDING TO AND TAKING FROM

Working in pairs or groups of three, students will solve addition and subtraction word problems within 20 involving situations of adding to and taking from. Students will use counters, create drawings, and write equations to represent the problems.

MATERIALS

20 counters for each pair or group of students; crayons; drawing paper; reproducible, "Addition and Subtraction Word Problems, I," for each student.

PROCEDURE

1. Hand out the materials. Explain that the reproducible has six word problems.

2. Explain that each pair or group of students is to read the problems. (You may find it beneficial if you read all of the problems together as a class at the beginning of the activity. Explain any words that students may not be familiar with.) Students are to discuss what each problem is asking them to find, and how they can solve the problem. Together, they should use the counters to model the problem. For example, to model 4 + 7, students would start with 4 counters and add 7 counters to show a sum of 11.

3. Explain that after they have represented a problem with counters, students are to work individually and create a drawing that represents the problem. They are also to write an equation with a symbol for the unknown number that represents the problem below their

drawing. For example, $4 + 7 = ?$. Then they are to write the equation with its solution: $4 + 7 = 11$. Students should solve all of the problems in this manner.

CLOSURE

Discuss the answers to the problems. Point out how the problems represent situations of adding to and taking from. Have volunteers share their drawings and equations with the class. Display your students' work.

ANSWERS

Each equation is followed by its solution. Drawings should illustrate the problem.
(1) $8 + 4 = ?$; 12 **(2)** $6 - 2 = ?$; 4 **(3)** $14 - ? = 8$; 6 **(4)** $12 + ? = 15$; 3 **(5)** $? + 6 = 17$; 11
(6) $? - 9 = 6$; 15

ACTIVITY 2: WORD PROBLEMS—PUTTING TOGETHER, TAKING APART, AND COMPARING

Working in pairs or groups of three, students will solve addition and subtraction word problems within 20 involving situations of putting together, taking apart, and comparing. Students will use counters, create drawings, and write equations to represent the problems.

MATERIALS

20 counters for each pair or group of students; crayons; drawing paper; reproducible, "Addition and Subtraction Word Problems, II," for each student.

PROCEDURE

1. Hand out the materials. Explain that the reproducible has six word problems.

2. Explain that each pair or group of students is to read the problems. (You may find it beneficial if you read all of the problems together as a class at the beginning of the activity. Explain any words that students may not be familiar with.) Students are to discuss what each problem is asking them to find, and how they can solve the problem. Together, they should use the counters to model the problem. For example, to model $12 - 7$, students would start with 12 counters and then take 7, leaving 5.

3. Explain that after they have represented each problem with counters, students are to work individually and create a drawing that represents the problem. They are also to write an equation with a symbol for the unknown number that represents the problem below their drawing, and then write the equation with its solution. For example, $12 - 7 = ?$ and $12 - 7 = 5$. They are to complete all of the problems in this manner.

CLOSURE

Discuss the answers to the problems and point out how the problems show putting together, taking apart, and comparing. Ask for volunteers to share their drawings and equations with the class. Display students' work.

ANSWERS

Equations may vary; one correct equation and its solution are provided for each problem. Drawings should illustrate the problem. **(1)** $10 + 6 = ?$; 16 **(2)** $7 + 8 = ?$; 15 **(3)** $11 + 9 = ?$; 20 **(4)** $12 - 8 = ?$; 4 **(5)** $10 - 9 = ?$; 1 **(6)** $16 - 11 = ?$; 5

ACTIVITY 3: ADDING WHEN BOTH ADDENDS ARE UNKNOWN

Working in pairs or groups of three, students will find how many of 20 counters can be put into two cups when both addends are unknown. They will use counters to find the addends and will represent the addends with equations and drawings. (Note: You may modify this activity by using fewer counters. You may also want to divide the activity into two or more sessions.)

MATERIALS

20 counters; 2 plastic cups (or similar containers); crayons; drawing paper for each pair or group of students; marker for the teacher.

PREPARATION

Label one plastic cup "1" and the another cup "2" for each pair or group of students. Place 20 counters in every cup 2.

PROCEDURE

1. Hand out the materials. Explain that each pair or group of students has 20 counters. Ask your students: How many of the counters can you put in cup 1 and cup 2?

2. Explain that there are many ways to do this. Tell your students that all 20 of their counters were passed out to them in cup 2. Ask: What equation could you write to show this? $20 = 0 + 20$.

3. Instruct your students to put all of their counters in cup 1. Ask: What equation could you write to show this?

$20 = 20 + 0$

4. Explain that students are to follow this procedure and find as many ways as they can to show how many counters can be put in cup 1 and how many counters can be put in cup 2, using all 20 counters. Suggest that they start with 1 counter in cup 1 and continue from there.

5. Explain that after finding a pair of addends, they are to draw the counters on their paper and write an equation that represents the addends.

CLOSURE

Discuss students' results. Ask volunteers to provide unknown addends for other numbers, for example, 7, 12, and 14, without using counters. (Allow students to use counters, if necessary.)

ANSWERS

Equations for pairs of addends are shown. Drawings should match the equations.

$20 = 0 + 20; 20 = 20 + 0$ $20 = 1 + 19; 20 = 19 + 1$ $20 = 2 + 18; 20 = 18 + 2$

$20 = 3 + 17; 20 = 17 + 3$ $20 = 4 + 16; 20 = 16 + 4$ $20 = 5 + 15; 20 = 15 + 5$

$20 = 6 + 14; 20 = 14 + 6$ $20 = 7 + 13; 20 = 13 + 7$ $20 = 8 + 12; 20 = 12 + 8$

$20 = 9 + 11; 20 = 11 + 9$ $20 = 10 + 10$

ADDITION AND SUBTRACTION WORD PROBLEMS, I

Directions: Solve the problems. Make a drawing and write an equation for each problem.

1. 8 birds were on a tree limb. 4 more birds landed on the limb. How many birds are on the limb now?

2. 6 kittens were asleep. 2 kittens woke up. How many kittens are still asleep?

3. 14 children sat at a table. Some children left. Then 8 students were at the table. How many children left?

4. 12 children were waiting for the school bus. Some more children came. Then there were 15 children. How many children came and waited with the first 12?

5. Some children waited in line for ice cream. 6 more children came. Then there were 17 children. How many children were waiting in line before?

6. Some cookies were on a dish. 9 cookies were eaten. Then there were 6 cookies on the dish. How many cookies were on the dish before?

Name _____

ADDITION AND SUBTRACTION WORD PROBLEMS, II

Directions: Solve the problems. Make a drawing and write an equation for each problem.

1. 10 ducks and 6 geese were on a pond. How many ducks and geese were on the pond?

2. John has 7 fewer toy trucks than Manny. John has 8 toy trucks. How many toy trucks does Manny have?

3. 11 red flowers and 9 white flowers are in a basket. How many flowers are in the basket?

4. Maria has 8 goldfish. Becky has 12 goldfish. How many more goldfish does Becky have than Maria?

5. Jacob has 9 fewer pencils than Annie. Annie has 10 pencils. How many pencils does Jacob have?

6. 16 deer were on a field. 11 were adults. The rest were fawns. How many were fawns?

Operations and Algebraic Thinking: 1.OA.2

"Represent and solve problems involving addition and subtraction."

2. "Solve word problems that call for addition of three whole numbers whose sum is less than or equal to 20, e.g., by using objects, drawings, and equations with a symbol for the unknown number to represent the problem."

BACKGROUND

To solve word problems efficiently, students must be able to read and understand the problem. They must identify the necessary information, decide what the problem is asking them to find, and do the math to find the answer. If any of these skills is lacking, students will have difficulty solving the problem and may become frustrated and anxious when asked to solve word problems.

ACTIVITY: WORD PROBLEMS WITH THREE ADDENDS

Students will be given a reproducible with five word problems. They will solve the problems by using counters, creating drawings, and writing equations.

MATERIALS

20 counters; crayons; reproducible, "Addition Word Problems," for each student.

PROCEDURE

1. Hand out the materials. Explain that the reproducible contains five problems that students are to solve.

2. Explain that students are to read each problem carefully. (You may find it beneficial if you read all of the problems together as a class at the beginning of the activity. Explain any words that students may not be familiar with.) For each problem students should do the following:

   • Decide what the problem is asking them to find.

   • Identify the information needed to solve the problem.

   • Use the necessary math skills to solve the problem.

   • Double-check their work for accuracy.

3. Explain that students should use counters to represent each problem. They should then draw objects such as small circles or pictures, write equations to represent the problem, and then solve the problem. Encourage your students to label the answers.

4. If necessary, explain that when adding three numbers, students might add the first two numbers, find a sum, and then add that sum to the third number. For example, to add $3 + 6 + 4$, students might add $3 + 6$ to find 9 and then add $9 + 4$ to find 13. Or they might add $6 + 4$ to find 10 and then add $10 + 3$ to find 13.

CLOSURE

Check students' answers. Discuss each problem and ask questions such as the following: How did you know what you were supposed to find? How did you know what information you needed to solve the problem? When double-checking your work, did you find an answer that was wrong? How did you correct it?

ANSWERS

Equations are followed by their answers. Drawings should match equations.
(1) $3 + 4 + 2 = ?$; 9 shirts **(2)** $7 + 3 + 6 = ?$; 16 trees **(3)** $5 + 4 + 11 = ?$; 20 animals
(4) $2 + 8 + 6 = ?$; 16 inches of snow **(5)** $8 + 8 + 3 = ?$; 19 counters

Name _____

ADDITION WORD PROBLEMS

Directions: Solve the problems. Make a drawing and write an equation for each problem.

1. Danny has 3 blue shirts, 4 green shirts, and 2 red shirts. How many shirts does Danny have?

2. There are 7 pine trees, 3 oak trees, and 6 maple trees in Jen's yard. How many trees are in her yard?

3. There are 5 horses, 4 cows, and 11 chickens on Mr. Smith's farm. How many animals are on his farm?

4. It snowed 2 inches on Monday. It snowed 8 inches on Thursday. It snowed 6 inches on Saturday. How much did it snow in all?

5. Emma used counters to solve a math problem. She had 8 red counters, 8 blue counters, and 3 green counters. How many counters did Emma have?

Operations and Algebraic Thinking: 1.OA.3

"Understand and apply properties of operations and the relationship between addition and subtraction."

> 3. "Apply properties of operations as strategies to add and subtract."

BACKGROUND

While students in first grade need not name or explain properties of operations, such as the commutative property of addition and the associative property of addition in formal terms, being able to apply these properties can help them add and subtract efficiently. An understanding of properties of operations enhances students' number sense and ability to compute, and lays the foundation for learning higher concepts in coming grades.

ACTIVITY: SPIN AND ADD

Working in pairs or groups of three, students will use spinners to find numbers to complete pairs of equations.

MATERIALS

1 spinner with the numbers 0 to 9 for each pair or group of students (number cards can be substituted); reproducible, "Addition Equations," for each student. (Note: Although spinners are available from many school supply companies, you may prefer to make spinners of your own. Many online sites offer instructions. A phrase such as "making a spinner for the classroom" will result in helpful Web sites.)

PROCEDURE

1. Hand out the materials. Explain that the reproducible contains eight rows of equations with each row having two equations. The equations have missing numbers.

2. Explain that students are to take turns and use the spinner to find an addend, or addends, to complete the first equation in each row. They are to then solve the equation and use the same numbers to make the second equation in the row true. Students should confer to complete the equations, and then each student is to complete his or her own reproducible.

3. Complete the two equations in the first row to make sure that everyone knows what to do. Ask a student to spin her spinner to find the missing addend in $7 + \underline{\hspace{1cm}} = \underline{\hspace{1cm}}$.

Suppose the student spins an 8. Students are to write 8 as the second addend in the first equation. Because $7 + 8 = 15$, they should write 15 after the equal sign. Next, using these numbers, they are to complete the second equation in the row, _____ $+ 7 =$ _____. They should write $8 + 7 = 15$, demonstrating the commutative property of addition. Point out that for row numbers 5 through 8, students must spin the spinner twice to find two addends for the first equation in each row.

4. Emphasize that students are to use their spinners to find the missing addend, or addends, only in the first equation of each pair of equations. They are to then solve the equation and then use the numbers to complete the second equation of the pair. They are to complete all of the equations.

CLOSURE

Check your students' work. Note that because students used spinners, their equations will vary. Have students share the equations they wrote with other students. Ask for volunteers to share some of their equations with the class by writing their equations in both forms on the board.

Name_____

ADDITION EQUATIONS

Directions: Use your spinner. Find the missing addend in each equation on the left. Solve the equation. Then use the numbers to complete the equation on the right.

1. $7 + \underline{\hspace{1cm}} = \underline{\hspace{1cm}}$ $\underline{\hspace{1cm}} + 7 = \underline{\hspace{1cm}}$

2. $\underline{\hspace{1cm}} + 5 = \underline{\hspace{1cm}}$ $5 + \underline{\hspace{1cm}} = \underline{\hspace{1cm}}$

3. $\underline{\hspace{1cm}} + 11 = \underline{\hspace{1cm}}$ $11 + \underline{\hspace{1cm}} = \underline{\hspace{1cm}}$

4. $10 + \underline{\hspace{1cm}} = \underline{\hspace{1cm}}$ $\underline{\hspace{1cm}} + 10 = \underline{\hspace{1cm}}$

5. $\underline{\hspace{1cm}} + \underline{\hspace{1cm}} + 2 = \underline{\hspace{1cm}}$ $\underline{\hspace{1cm}} + 2 = \underline{\hspace{1cm}}$

6. $1 + \underline{\hspace{1cm}} + \underline{\hspace{1cm}} = \underline{\hspace{1cm}}$ $1 + \underline{\hspace{1cm}} = \underline{\hspace{1cm}}$

7. $\underline{\hspace{1cm}} + 0 + \underline{\hspace{1cm}} = \underline{\hspace{1cm}}$ $\underline{\hspace{1cm}} + 0 = \underline{\hspace{1cm}}$

8. $\underline{\hspace{1cm}} + 2 + \underline{\hspace{1cm}} = \underline{\hspace{1cm}}$ $\underline{\hspace{1cm}} + 2 = \underline{\hspace{1cm}}$

Operations and Algebraic Thinking: 1.OA.4

"Understand and apply properties of operations and the relationship between addition and subtraction."

> 4. "Understand subtraction as an unknown-addend problem."

BACKGROUND

Once students understand that subtraction can be viewed as an unknown-addend problem, they can see that addition and subtraction are related. This understanding makes it clear that addition and subtraction are inverse operations. For example, $11 - 5 = 6$ is the inverse of $5 + 6 = 11$.

 ### ACTIVITY: FINDING UNKNOWN ADDENDS

Working in pairs or groups of three, students will use cards and dice to write subtraction problems and related unknown-addend problems.

MATERIALS

Scissors; 2 dice (each numbered 1 to 6); reproducible, "Subtraction Cards (12 to 20)," for each pair or group of students. Optional: 20 counters for each pair or group of students.

PROCEDURE

1. Explain that subtraction problems can be rewritten as addition problems. For example, to subtract $14 - 6$, students can find the number that makes 14 when added to 6: $6 + \_\_\_ = 14; 6 + 8 = 14$, so $14 - 6 = 8$.

2. Hand out the materials. (If you feel that your students will find counters helpful, hand out the counters as well.) Explain that the reproducible has 16 cards with the numbers 12 to 20. Some numbers appear on two cards.

3. Explain that students are to cut out each of the cards. They are to mix up the cards and place them in a pile.

4. Explain the exercise. A student takes a card. This card becomes the first number of a subtraction problem. The student then rolls the dice. The number rolled becomes the number to subtract.

5. Provide the following example for the class to do together. Assume that the card a student picked was 15 and the number rolled with the dice was 9. The subtraction problem is

15 − 9. Students are to record this problem on a sheet of paper. They are to solve the problem by rewriting it as an addition problem. They should record this on their paper as 9 + _____ = 15 next to the subtraction problem. The unknown addend is 6, which is also the answer to 15 − 9. Students should record this on their paper. (If you handed out counters, encourage students to use their counters to help them find the answers to the problems.)

6. Instruct your students to take turns picking cards and rolling the dice to create more problems. You may instruct students to keep working until they pick all of the cards, or you may have them pick a given number of cards. You may also have students do another round.

CLOSURE

Check your students' work. Ask volunteers to share some of their equations, which you should write on the board. Discuss how each subtraction problem can be solved by rewriting it as an addition problem. Remind your students of the relationship between subtraction and addition.

16	17	12	15
14	13	18	13
15	17	16	19
20	18	19	14

Operations and Algebraic Thinking: 1.OA.5

"Add and subtract within 20."

5. "Relate counting to addition and subtraction (e.g., by counting on 2 to add 2)."

BACKGROUND

Addition and subtraction are related to counting. For example, when you add 5 to a number, you are actually counting the next five numbers in succession from the number to which you are adding the 5. When you subtract 5 from a number, you are counting backward from the number. This can be easily demonstrated on a grid, using counters.

 ACTIVITY: COUNTING FORWARD AND BACKWARD

Working in pairs or groups of three, students will use the number cards from standard decks of cards, counters, and a grid to demonstrate that adding a number is the same as counting forward and that subtracting a number is the same as counting backward. Students will write number sentences to record their work.

MATERIALS

2 suits of standard playing cards (ace to 10); 20 counters; reproducible, "Counting Number Grid," for each pair or group of students; reproducible, "Count On: Add or Subtract," for each student.

PREPARATION

Remove the jokers and face cards (leaving the ace to 10) for two suits of cards for each pair or group of students. Provide a red suit (hearts or diamonds) and a black suit (spades or clubs) for each pair or group.

PROCEDURE

1. Hand out the materials. Explain that each pair or group of students has two suits of cards (preferably a red suit and a black suit). The cards range from ace to 10 with the ace representing the number 1. Tell students to keep each suit in a different pile. The reproducible, "Counting Number Grid," contains a grid showing the numbers from 1 to 20. The other reproducible, "Count On: Add or Subtract," contains number sentences that students will complete, using their cards.

2. Explain that addition and subtraction are related to counting. Offer this example of addition: $8 + 3 = 11$ is related to counting 3 forward from 8, which results in 11. Instruct your students to place a counter on each number from 1 to 8 on their grid. They should now place counters on the next three numbers, 9, 10, and 11. The last counter, placed on 11, shows that $8 + 3$ and counting 3 forward from 8 both equal 11. Now provide this example of subtraction: $8 - 3 = 5$. Instruct your students to show this problem on their grid. They should place a counter on each number from 1 to 8 on their grid. Starting with 8, they should count back and remove 3 counters from 8, one each from 8, 7, and 6. This leaves counters on 1 to 5, which shows that $8 - 3$ and counting back 3 from 8 both equal 5.

3. Explain that students are to use their materials to show other examples that relate counting to addition and subtraction. After mixing up their cards and placing them face down (being sure to keep the suits separate), they should follow these steps:

   - Pick a card from one of the suits of cards. Then pick a card from the other suit.

   - Write the larger number on their reproducible, "Count On: Add or Subtract," in the first space of a number sentence.

   - Starting with number 1, place a counter on each number of the grid up to and including the larger number.

   - Write the smaller number in the second space of the same number sentence.

   - For addition, count from the larger number on the grid and place a counter on each successive number to represent the smaller number. (For example, to show $5 + 3$, first place counters on the numbers 1 through 5 on the grid, and then place 3 more counters, one each on the numbers 6, 7, and 8.)

   - For subtraction, count backward from the larger number and remove counters that represent the smaller number. (For example, to show $5 - 3$, first place counters on the numbers 1 through 5 on the grid, and then remove 3 counters, one each from the numbers 5, 4, and 3. The remaining counters on numbers 1 and 2 show that $5 - 3 = 2$.) If all counters are removed from the grid, for example to show $5 - 5$, the answer is zero.

   - Complete the number sentence by writing the number covered by the last counter, or zero if no counters are left.

4. Explain that students are to continue in the same way: pick pairs of cards, use counters to model addition and subtraction by counting on their grid, and complete the number sentences. Although students are to work together picking cards and using counters on the grid, each is to complete his or her own number sentences.

CLOSURE

Check your students' results, which will vary. Ask volunteers to explain how some of their number sentences can be modeled on the grid. As they explain their work, have other students model the examples of counting forward and backward on their own grids.

1	2	3	4	5
6	7	8	9	10
11	12	13	14	15
16	17	18	19	20

Name _____

COUNT ON: ADD OR SUBTRACT

Directions: Complete the number sentences.

1) _____ + _____ = _____

2) _____ − _____ = _____

3) _____ + _____ = _____

4) _____ − _____ = _____

5) _____ + _____ = _____

6) _____ − _____ = _____

7) _____ + _____ = _____

8) _____ − _____ = _____

9) _____ + _____ = _____

10) _____ − _____ = _____

Operations and Algebraic Thinking: 1.OA.6

"Add and subtract within 20."

> 6. "Add and subtract within 20, demonstrating fluency for addition and subtraction within 10. Use strategies such as counting on; making ten (e.g., $8 + 6 = 8 + 2 + 4 = 10 + 4 = 14$); decomposing a number leading to a ten (e.g., $13 - 4 = 13 - 3 - 1 = 10 - 1 = 9$); using the relationship between addition and subtraction (e.g., knowing that $8 + 4 = 12$, one knows that $12 - 8 = 4$); and creating equivalent but easier or known sums (e.g., adding $6 + 7$ by creating the known equivalent $6 + 6 + 1 = 12 + 1 = 13$)."

BACKGROUND

As students acquire various strategies for adding and subtracting, their fluency with these operations increases. Knowing and being able to apply different strategies for finding answers to addition and subtraction problems broadens students' general understanding of the relationships of operations and reinforces their computational skills.

ACTIVITY 1: ADDITION AND SUBTRACTION BINGO

Students receive a bingo board on which they will randomly write the numbers 0 to 20. After the teacher presents an addition or subtraction problem, students solve the problem, then find the answer on their bingo board, and cover the answer with a counter. The first student to cover five squares in a row, column, or along a diagonal wins.

MATERIALS

25 counters; reproducible, "Addition and Subtraction Bingo," for each student. Optional: Reproducible, "Addition and Subtraction Bingo Problems," for the teacher.

PROCEDURE

1. Explain that students are to play a game called bingo. In this game, which is a little different from the standard game of bingo, you will present addition and subtraction problems that students will solve. Students will then find the answers to the problems on their bingo boards.

2. Hand out the materials. Explain that the bingo board contains 25 squares. At the bottom of the board are the numbers 0 to 20.

3. Explain that students are to randomly pick four spaces in different rows and columns, excluding spaces on diagonals, and write the words "Free Space" on them. (You may instead simply have students place an "X" on each of these spaces.) Be sure that your students understand what "row," "column," and "diagonal" mean, and that "randomly" means no special order. Next, students are to randomly write each number from 0 to 20 in one of the remaining spaces on their board. As they write a number, they should cross it out on the bottom of the page so that they do not mistakenly use the number again. All numbers will be used. After they finish writing the numbers on their boards, they should place a counter on each free space.

4. Explain the rules of the game. You will announce a problem. (You may also write it on the board.) Suggest that students write the problem on paper and use whichever strategies they wish to solve the problem. For example, they may count on, make ten, decompose numbers, use easier sums, or use the relationship between addition and subtraction. Some of your students may be able to find the answers mentally for easy problems.

5. Explain that once students have solved a problem, they are to find the answer on their bingo board and place a counter on that space. The first student who covers five spaces in a row, column, or along a diagonal is the winner. When a student has bingo, she should raise her hand and say "Bingo!" Tell the other students not to remove their counters until you check that the answers are correct.

6. Start the game. Use the problems from "Addition and Subtraction Bingo Problems," which you may copy if you prefer. Note that the answers are included with the problems. In case no one gets bingo after you have used all of the problems, you may declare the student (or students) who had the most counters in a row, column, or along a diagonal the winner. You may play additional games on the same board by presenting the problems in a different order, or by creating problems of your own, being sure that the sums and differences are within 20.

CLOSURE

Discuss the game. Ask your students what strategies they used to solve the problems. Ask them to write an addition or subtraction problem that would have resulted in the answer, or answers, they needed for bingo. Even the winner can do this by writing problems that would have resulted in answers that would have given him bingo in another way.

 ## ACTIVITY 2: ADDITION AND SUBTRACTION USING TENS

Working in groups, students will create addition and subtraction problems by making 10 and decomposing a number leading to 10. They will share their work with the class, explaining the strategies they used to assemble and solve the problems.

Scissors; rulers; glue sticks; construction paper; reproducible, "Addition and Subtraction Equations with 10," for each group of students.

PROCEDURE

1. Explain to your students that addition and subtraction problems can be solved in many ways. Review that one of these ways is to make one of the numbers a 10, or decompose (break down) a number leading to 10. Adding or subtracting with a 10 can be easier than adding or subtracting other numbers. Provide examples, such as the following:

   - Addition: $9 + 6 = 9 + 1 + 5 = 10 + 5 = 15$. Explain the steps, showing how 6 is rewritten as $1 + 5$, and then the 1 is added to the 9 to make 10. Adding $10 + 5$ is the same as adding $9 + 6$. Both equal 15.

   - Subtraction: $14 - 8 = 14 - 4 - 4 = 10 - 4 = 6$. Explain the steps, showing how 8 is rewritten as two 4s. Taking the first 4 from 14 leaves $10 - 4$ and results in the same answer as $14 - 8$. Both equal 6.

2. Hand out the materials. Explain that the reproducible contains cards with equations, or partial equations.

3. Instruct your students to cut out the title of the reproducible and then cut out the cards.

4. Explain that students are to arrange the cards to show the steps for making 10 to solve two addition problems and to show the steps for decomposing, or breaking down, a number leading to a 10 to solve two subtraction problems. They are to then glue the cards on their construction paper showing the problems and how each one can be rewritten using 10. Students should also glue the title on the top of their construction paper.

5. To demonstrate what they are to do, complete a problem together as a class. Tell your students to start with $6 + 8 =$. Ask them what the next step would be to rewrite the problem making a 10. It would be the card that has $6 + 4 + 4 =$. Now ask how they could make a 10 and complete the addition problem. They should realize it would be the card with $10 + 4 = 14$. Students should now glue these cards in a row on their construction paper. Suggest that they use their ruler to keep the row straight. They are to follow the same steps to create another addition problem and two subtraction problems.

6. Encourage your students to discuss and arrange all of the cards to show problems making 10 and decomposing a number leading to a 10 before gluing the cards on their papers.

CLOSURE

Have your students present their work to the class. Ask volunteers of each group to explain the strategies their group used to arrange the cards correctly to create the problems.

The completed problems follow:

$$6 + 8 = 6 + 4 + 4 = 10 + 4 = 14$$

$$8 + 5 = 8 + 2 + 3 = 10 + 3 = 13$$

$$15 - 6 = 15 - 5 - 1 = 10 - 1 = 9$$

$$11 - 8 = 11 - 1 - 7 = 10 - 7 = 3$$

		Bingo Board		

Number Bank

0	1	2	3	4	5	6
7	8	9	10	11	12	13
14	15	16	17	18	19	20

ADDITION AND SUBTRACTION BINGO PROBLEMS

(1) $7 + 11 = 18$

(2) $9 - 2 = 7$

(3) $6 + 3 = 9$

(4) $4 + 4 = 8$

(5) $13 - 10 = 3$

(6) $15 - 5 = 10$

(7) $6 + 9 = 15$

(8) $7 - 7 = 0$

(9) $3 + 2 = 5$

(10) $7 + 7 = 14$

(11) $12 - 8 = 4$

(12) $19 - 3 = 16$

(13) $6 + 5 = 11$

(14) $13 + 4 = 17$

(15) $6 - 5 = 1$

(16) $12 - 10 = 2$

(17) $14 - 2 = 12$

(18) $11 + 9 = 20$

(19) $10 - 4 = 6$

(20) $6 + 7 = 13$

(21) $6 + 13 = 19$

Addition and Subtraction Equations with 10

$8 + 5 =$	$10 - 1 = 9$	$11 - 8 =$
$6 + 4 + 4 =$	$15 - 5 - 1 =$	$10 - 7 = 3$
$6 + 8 =$	$15 - 6 =$	$10 + 4 = 14$
$10 + 3 = 13$	$11 - 1 - 7 =$	$8 + 2 + 3 =$

Operations and Algebraic Thinking: 1.OA.7

"Work with addition and subtraction equations."

> 7. "Understand the meaning of the equal sign, and determine if equations involving addition and subtraction are true or false."

BACKGROUND

To understand equations, students must understand the meaning of the equal sign. Knowing that numbers on both sides of an equal sign have the same value is a basic concept in math and is the foundation for working with equations.

 ACTIVITY: TRUE OR FALSE EQUATIONS GAME

Working in pairs or groups of three, students will play a game in which they pick cards containing equations and determine if the equations are true or false. Students receive 1 point for each correct answer and no points for incorrect answers. The student with the most points at the end of the game wins.

MATERIALS

Scissors; reproducible, "True or False Equation Cards," for each pair or group of students; reproducible, "True or False Equation Game Score Sheet," for each student.

PROCEDURE

1. Explain that an equal sign is a symbol that means the numbers to each side of it have the same value. This number sentence is called an equation. Following are some examples of equations: $5 = 5, 3 + 2 = 2 + 3$, and $4 - 1 = 2 + 1$.

2. Hand out the materials. Explain that the reproducible "True or False Equation Cards" contains cards with equations numbered 1 to 18. Students are to cut out the cards, mix them up, and place them face down in a pile. The reproducible "True or False Equation Game Score Sheet" is a sheet for each student to keep his or her score.

3. Explain the rules of the game. Students are to take turns and pick a card. (In the case of a group, each student takes a turn and plays against the other two.) The student who picks a card must decide if the equation on it is true or false. After she decides, she tells her opponent. She then writes "True" or "False" next to the number of the card on her score sheet. The cards will not be chosen in order, and students must write their answer on the

line next to the card's number. During the course of the game, they will not write answers for all of the cards.

4. Explain that after a student announces whether an equation is true or false, her opponent can challenge the answer if he believes it is wrong. He would then write the card number and his answer on the line under "Challenges" on his score sheet. Challenge answers cannot be the same as an opponent's original answer.

5. Explain the scoring. Players receive 1 point for each correct answer and no points for wrong answers. They receive 1 point for each correct challenge answer, but they lose a point if a challenge answer they wrote is incorrect. Emphasize to your students that they should only write a challenge answer if they are sure their opponent's answer is wrong. While writing correct challenge answers result in higher scores, incorrect challenge answers lower scores.

6. Do a sample round. On the board, write an equation: $1 + 4 = 2 + 3$. Ask a volunteer if this is true or false. It is true. If a student had picked this card, he would write "True" next to problem 1 on his score sheet. But if his opponent thought the answer was wrong, the opponent would challenge his answer and write the number 1 (for problem 1) and "False" under "Challenges" on her own score sheet. At the end of the game, when you announce the correct answers, the student who marked this equation as true receives 1 point but the student who challenged incorrectly loses 1 point.

7. Start the game. Remind students to record their answers on their score sheets.

CLOSURE

Announce the answers to the game and discuss corrections for the equations that were false. Have students tally their scores by adding 1 point for each correct answer, including challenge answers. But they must subtract 1 point for each incorrect challenge answer they wrote. Instruct your students to write one equation that is true and one that is false, and exchange their equations for the equations of a partner. Students should identify each other's true and false equations.

ANSWERS

(1) True (2) True (3) False (4) True (5) True (6) False (7) True (8) False (9) False (10) True
(11) False (12) False (13) True (14) False (15) True (16) False (17) True (18) False

1) $9 = 9$	2) $3 + 1 = 1 + 3$	3) $7 = 5$
4) $0 = 0$	5) $4 + 2 = 5 + 1$	6) $8 + 1 = 9 - 1$
7) $8 = 6 + 2$	8) $5 - 2 = 7 - 3$	9) $10 = 3 + 4$
10) $4 + 5 = 10 - 1$	11) $2 + 8 = 9 - 3$	12) $0 + 5 = 6$
13) $12 = 6 + 6$	14) $4 + 4 = 10 - 3$	15) $3 + 8 = 8 + 3$
16) $3 + 6 = 12 - 4$	17) $6 + 7 = 13$	18) $11 - 6 = 3 + 4$

Name_____

TRUE OR FALSE EQUATION GAME SCORE SHEET

Directions: Write True or False for each equation card.

1) _____   10) _____

2) _____   11) _____

3) _____   12) _____

4) _____   13) _____

5) _____   14) _____

6) _____   15) _____

7) _____   16) _____

8) _____   17) _____

9) _____   18) _____

Challenges: Write the number of the equation. Then write True or False.

_____

_____

Operations and Algebraic Thinking: 1.OA.8

"Work with addition and subtraction equations."

8. "Determine the unknown whole number in an addition or subtraction equation relating three whole numbers."

BACKGROUND

To determine unknown numbers in an addition or subtraction equation, students must understand not only that numbers on opposite sides of the equal symbol have the same value, but also the relationship between addition and subtraction. Mastery of these concepts leads to proficiency when adding and subtracting.

 ACTIVITY: ADDITION AND SUBTRACTION EQUATIONS GAME

Working in pairs or groups of three, students will play a game that is a takeoff on tic-tac-toe. This game is played on an expanded board and students must solve addition and subtraction equations to win.

MATERIALS

Scissors; reproducibles, "Addition and Subtraction Equations Game Board" and "Addition and Subtraction Equation Cards," for each pair or group of students; 10 counters for each student. (For each pair or group of students, each set of 10 counters should be a different color or shape. For example, one student might have red counters and the other student might have yellow counters.)

PROCEDURE

1. Explain that students will play an addition and subtraction equation game. The game is somewhat similar to tic-tac-toe.

2. Hand out the materials. Explain that the reproducible "Addition and Subtraction Equations Game Board" contains 20 spaces with a number in each space. Reproducible "Addition and Subtraction Equation Cards" contains 20 equations. Students are to cut the equation cards out, mix them up, and place them face down.

3. Explain the rules of the game. Students are to take turns and pick one card at a time. (In the case of a group of three, all students play, taking turns one at a time. A third set of counters of a different color will be needed.) The student who picked the card is to solve

the equation. He is to then find the answer on the game board and place one of his counters on it. The next student then picks a card and follows the same procedure. Students should write their answer on each of their equation cards and keep their cards in a separate pile. This makes it easier to verify answers at the end of the game. (Note: If you wish to play more than one game, have students write equations and answers on a separate sheet of paper so that the equation cards can be used again.)

4. Explain that if a student picks a card and solves an equation, but her opponent previously placed a counter incorrectly on that answer, she may place her own counter on that answer next to her opponent's counter and write the answer on her equation card.

5. Explain that students can win the game in one of two ways. The first way is for a student to get three counters consecutively in a row, column, or diagonal. (The entire row, column, or diagonal does not have to be covered with the same colored counters.) Make sure that your students understand what "row," "column," and "diagonal" mean. The second way is to complete all of the equations without anyone placing three counters in a row. In this case, the student with the most counters on correct answers is the winner.

6. Start the game. Note that even if one of the players gets three counters in a row, students should play until all of the cards have been used so that the winner can be verified. You can play more games by creating and presenting equations of your own, making sure that the answers to the equations are on the game board.

CLOSURE

After everyone has finished solving all the equations, announce the answers. Suggest that students place their equations in front of them in numerical order so that they can match equations with the answers. (This will be especially helpful in the case of incorrect answers.) Ask if anyone got three answers in a row. Ask who won in each group and how many games ended in a tie. Discuss any equations students had trouble with. Have volunteers explain the strategies they used to find the answers to specific equations.

ANSWERS

(1) 4 **(2)** 7 **(3)** 10 **(4)** 2 **(5)** 8 **(6)** 0 **(7)** 12 **(8)** 6 **(9)** 5 **(10)** 9 **(11)** 3 **(12)** 13 **(13)** 15 **(14)** 1 **(15)** 17 **(16)** 18 **(17)** 19 **(18)** 14 **(19)** 16 **(20)** 11

7	11	8	12
1	15	18	2
4	0	10	6
9	17	14	3
16	5	19	13

1) $9 - 5 = ?$	2) $2 + ? = 9$	3) $? = 3 + 7$	4) $? + 8 = 10$
5) $? = 16 - 8$	6) $7 - 7 = ?$	7) $? + 5 = 17$	8) $14 - ? = 8$
9) $5 + ? = 10$	10) $14 = ? + 5$	11) $16 - ? = 13$	12) $18 = ? + 5$
13) $5 + 10 = ?$	14) $? = 6 - 5$	15) $19 - 2 = ?$	16) $? = 9 + 9$
17) $? - 12 = 7$	18) $9 + 5 = ?$	19) $9 = ? - 7$	20) $18 - ? = 7$

Number and Operations in Base Ten: 1.NBT.1

"Extend the counting sequence."

1. "Count to 120, starting at any number less than 120. In this range, read and write numerals and represent a number of objects with a written numeral."

BACKGROUND

As students progress through first grade, they should master counting, reading, and writing numerals to 120. Competency with these skills is essential to understanding place value, which is the basis of our number system.

 ### ACTIVITY 1: SPIN AND COUNT

Working in groups, students will use spinners to create numbers and then count from those numbers to 120.

MATERIALS

A spinner with numbers 0 to 9 for each group.

PROCEDURE

1. Hand out the spinners. Explain that students will use the spinners to find numbers from which they will count to 120.

2. Explain that students will take turns in their groups. Each student will spin the spinner two times to find a two-digit number. The first number will represent the first digit (tens) and the second number will represent the second digit (ones). For example, if the first spin lands on 6 and the second spin lands on 2, the number to start counting from is 62. The student will now count aloud from 62 to 120. If the first spin lands on 0, and the second spin lands on 7, the number to start counting from is 7. If two spins land on 0, the student should start counting from 0 (or you might instead have them spin two more times).

3. Explain that as a student is counting, the other members of his group are to silently count along. If the student counting aloud makes a mistake, the other students should raise their hands to stop the count and offer the correct number, after which the student continues counting. You should correct any confusion.

4. Explain that after a student counts to 120, another student of the group spins two times to find a number and then counts from that number to 120. The procedure continues in this

way until all students have had a chance. If time permits, you may have students complete another round.

CLOSURE

Lead the class in counting from 1 to 120.

ACTIVITY 2: CALL OUT

You call out random numbers that students write on dry-erase boards.

MATERIALS

1 dry-erase board; 1 dry-erase marker; 1 eraser or dry-erase cloth for each student.

PROCEDURE

1. Hand out the materials. Explain that you will randomly call out a number that students are to write on their dry-erase boards. The numbers will not be in order.

2. Explain that after writing the number, students are to hold up their boards so that you can see what number they wrote.

3. Call out numbers one at a time. You may simply call out random numbers, or you may use the following list: 21, 35, 89, 75, 42, 63, 91, 114, 57, 19, 48, 78, 107, 81, and 50. You can, of course, add more numbers to provide students with more practice.

CLOSURE

Call out some random numbers, one at a time. First have students write the number on their dry-erase boards. Then ask for a volunteer to start counting forward from that number. After the student has counted 5 or 10 numbers, have another student continue counting. Follow this procedure until students count to 120. Repeat with a few more numbers.

ACTIVITY 3: DRAW AND COUNT

Working first individually and then in groups of up to six, students will draw objects, write the number that represents them, and then combine their drawn objects with the objects of the other students in their group for a total of up to 120. Students will write the number that represents the total.

Scissors; crayons; markers; glue stick; half-sheet of unlined $8\frac{1}{2}$-inch by 11-inch paper for each student; 1 sheet of poster paper or 1 sheet of 24-inch by 36-inch construction paper for each group.

PREPARATION

Cut sheets of unlined paper in half so that each student can receive half a sheet.

PROCEDURE

1. Explain to your students that, working individually, they will draw and color up to 20 objects of their choice on their unlined paper. They can decide the number and type of objects to draw. For example, they may draw 5 kittens, 11 triangles, or 20 stars—their choices are limited only by their imaginations.

2. Explain that they should draw their objects so that the objects fit neatly on their unlined paper. After they draw and color their objects, they are to write the number that represents them to the right of their objects.

3. After everyone has finished drawing, organize your students into groups of up to six. Explain that they are to work with their group members and glue the papers containing their objects onto the group's construction paper. Next they should count all of the objects and write the total number of all the objects on their construction paper.

CLOSURE

Have each group share their work with the class, pointing out the objects each group member drew and the number that represents their objects, as well as the total number of objects.

Number and Operations in Base Ten: 1.NBT.2

"Understand place value."

2. "Understand that the two digits of a two-digit number represent amounts of tens and ones. Understand the following as special cases:

a. "10 can be thought of as a bundle of ten ones—called a 'ten.'

b. "The numbers from 11 to 19 are composed of a ten and one, two, three, four, five, six, seven, eight, or nine ones.

c. "The numbers 10, 20, 30, 40, 50, 60, 70, 80, 90 refer to one, two, three, four, five, six, seven, eight, or nine tens (and 0 ones)."

BACKGROUND

Place value is an underlying concept to our number system. While a single-digit whole number represents ones, a two-digit whole number represents a value made of tens and ones. For example, 28 is composed of 2 tens and 8 ones.

ACTIVITY 1: NUMBERS AND GRIDS

The teacher presents students with two-digit numbers that they must represent in color on grid paper.

MATERIALS

Crayons; 2 sheets of reproducible, "100-Unit Grids," for each student.

PROCEDURE

1. Explain to your students that a two-digit number represents a value of tens and ones. For example, 35 is composed of 3 tens and 5 ones.

2. Hand out the materials. Explain that each sheet of grid paper has two grids of 100 squares, 10 across and 10 down. Each column and each row can represent 1 ten and each square can represent 1 one.

3. Explain that you will present numbers to your students that they are to represent on their grid paper. Do the following example together as a class. Ask your students how they could represent the number 12 on the grid. Students should realize that 12 can be shown as

1 column of ten and 2 more squares on another column. Instruct them to show 12 by coloring all 10 squares in one column and two squares in the next column. Have a volunteer count the total squares colored.

4. Present the following (or similar) numbers—15, 18, and 60—and instruct your students to represent each number on a grid. Caution students to be accurate in their work. They should write the numeral to the right of the squares they colored on each grid.

CLOSURE

Have students share their work with a friend to verify each other's results. Display your students' work.

ANSWERS

For 15, one column or row of 10 and 5 squares on the next column or row should be colored. For 18, one column or row of 10 and 8 squares on the next column or row should be colored. For 60, six columns or rows of 10 should be colored.

 ## ACTIVITY 2: VIRTUAL BASE BLOCKS AND PLACE VALUE

Using a Web site, the teacher will lead this activity in which students represent numbers with base blocks.

MATERIALS

Computer with Internet access; digital projector for the teacher.

PROCEDURE

1. Explain that place value is the value of each digit in a number, based on the digit's location, or place. For example, in the number 56, the 5 represents 5 tens, or 50, and the 6 represents 6 ones, or 6.

2. Go to http://nlvm.usu.edu/. Click on "Pre-K–2," "Numbers and Operations," and then click on "Base Blocks." You will find columns with virtual base ten blocks at the top. At the right of the screen, you will see a "Clear" button; at the bottom right you will see a "Show a Problem" button and up/down arrows to change the columns. Click on the down arrow next to "Columns" and set the screen to two columns. Once you have two columns, note that the rectangular block on the top of the left column represents tens and the cube on the next column represents ones. Clicking on either block shows a visual representation of the number, which is also shown in a numeral at the right of the screen. For example,

you can show 20 by clicking on the rectangular block twice; you can show 25 by clicking on the rectangular block twice and the cube 5 times. You can move blocks in the columns close to each other by clicking and dragging. Clicking on "New Problem" shows a number that can be represented with the blocks. To remove a block, simply drag it to the trash can on the lower right of the screen.

3. Do a sample problem together as a class. Click on "Show a Problem." Ask your students how they could represent this number using the blocks. They should name the number of tens and ones that show the problem. Clicking on the blocks will show a visual representation of the number.

4. Present several problems to your students, asking them how they would show the number with blocks.

CLOSURE

Ask volunteers to suggest a number and tell you how many blocks will be needed to represent it. Click on the necessary blocks to represent and verify their answer.

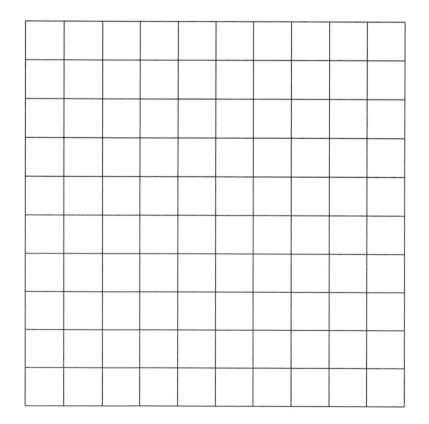

Number and Operations in Base Ten: 1.NBT.3

"Understand place value."

> 3. "Compare two two-digit numbers based on meanings of the tens and ones digits, recording the results of comparisons with the symbols >, =, and <."

BACKGROUND

By first grade, many students already have acquired basic understanding of comparing one-digit numbers. If you ask your students which team won a baseball game in which the score was 5 to 4, many will, without hesitation, tell you it was the team that scored 5 runs. As they learn the meaning of the tens and ones digits, they are able to extend comparisons to two-digit numbers.

 ACTIVITY: NUMBERS WAR GAME

Working in pairs or groups of three, students will use spinners to compare numbers using the symbols >, =, and <. The student with the higher number scores 1 point. At the end of the game, the student with the higher point total wins.

MATERIALS

1 spinner with the numbers 0 to 9 (1 decahedra die with the numbers 0 to 9 can be used instead) for each pair or group of students; 1 or 2 copies of reproducible, "Numbers War Game Score Sheet," for each student.

PROCEDURE

1. Review the meanings of the inequality symbols and equal sign with your students:

   >   means "is greater than."   8 > 7
   =   means "is equal to."   4 = 4
   <   means "is less than."   3 < 9

2. Depending on the abilities of your students, you may also find it helpful to review place value. For example, 25 is composed of 2 tens and 5 ones. Provide more examples if necessary.

3. Hand out the materials. Explain that students will play a Numbers War Game. Students play against each other, using spinners to create the numbers that they will compare.

4. Explain the rules of the game. Students take turns, with each student spinning the spinner twice. The first number the spinner lands on represents the tens. The second number represents the ones. For example, if a student spins a 7 and a 4, her number is 74. After the first student spins two times, the second student spins twice. Again, the first number spun represents the tens and the second number represents the ones. Students then compare their numbers. The student whose number was greater gets 1 point and the student with the lower number receives no point. If the numbers are equal, both students receive 1 point. The game continues following the same procedure. Note that if a student spins a 0 on her first spin, there will be no tens in her number. If she spins a second 0, her number is 0. (If three students are working together, students take turns playing against each other. Student A and Student B play, Student C and Student A play, Student C and Student B play, and then Student A and Student B play again, with the game continuing in this manner.)

5. Explain that after students spin and compare their numbers, they are to record their number on their own score sheet by writing an inequality or equality statement, starting with the first two-digit number spun on the round. Students should also mark a 1 under "Points" if the number they spun was the higher number, or 0 if the number they spun was the lower number. For equal numbers, each student receives 1 point and they should both mark their score sheets accordingly.

6. Begin the game. If students run out of room on their score sheets and the game is still being played, provide them with another sheet.

CLOSURE

Have students tally their scores by counting the points they scored. Check your students' work. Ask volunteers to share some of the comparisons they found and write them on the board for other students to see.

Name _____

NUMBERS WAR GAME SCORE SHEET

Directions: Compare numbers. Use >, =, and <.

First Two-Digit Number	>, =, <	Second Two-Digit Number	Points
_____	_____	_____	_____
_____	_____	_____	_____
_____	_____	_____	_____
_____	_____	_____	_____
_____	_____	_____	_____
_____	_____	_____	_____
_____	_____	_____	_____
_____	_____	_____	_____
_____	_____	_____	_____
_____	_____	_____	_____
_____	_____	_____	_____

Number and Operations in Base Ten: 1.NBT.4

"Use place value understanding and properties of operations to add and subtract."

> 4. "Add within 100, including adding a two-digit number and a one-digit number, and adding a two-digit number and a multiple of 10, using concrete models or drawings and strategies based on place value, properties of operations, and/or the relationship between addition and subtraction; relate the strategy to a written method and explain the reasoning used. Understand that in adding two-digit numbers, one adds tens and tens, ones and ones; and sometimes it is necessary to compose a ten."

BACKGROUND

To add two-digit numbers within 100 proficiently, students must understand place value. They must realize that they are adding tens and tens and ones and ones. Once they have mastered this skill, learning to add larger numbers is easier because the steps are similar.

ACTIVITY 1: READING ABOUT ADDITION

The teacher reads *Mission: Addition* by Loreen Leedy to the class.

MATERIALS

Mission: Addition by Loreen Leedy (Scholastic, 1998).

PROCEDURE

1. Gather your students around you so that you can share the illustrations with them as you read the book. Explain that you are going to read a book that is all about addition.

2. As you read, pause often and share the pictures with your students. Be sure to show the addition equations that are included in the book.

3. Emphasize the math vocabulary, such as *addend* and *sum*. Also emphasize concepts, such as changing the order of addends does not change the sum, and, how, when adding tens and ones, the ones are added first and kept in the ones column, and then the tens are added and kept in the tens column.

4. Ask your students to find the sums to the addition problems in the book, and to answer questions that are posed to the reader.

Discuss the book with your students and review the meanings of *addend* and *sum*. Ask volunteers to explain the steps for adding one-digit numbers and the steps for adding a two-digit number and a one-digit number.

ACTIVITY 2: ADDING AND VERIFYING SUMS

Students are given addition problems to solve, and they verify their sums on a grid.

MATERIALS

Crayons; 2 copies of reproducible, "100-Unit Grids" (located at the end of the activities for Standard 1.NBT.2), for each student.

PROCEDURE

1. Distribute the materials. Explain that each sheet of grid paper contains two grids, each with 100 square units.

2. Explain that you will write four problems on the board. Students are to add the problems and then verify their answers by coloring squares on their grid.

3. Present the following (or similar) problems to your students: (**1**) 32 + 7; (**2**) 53 + 5; (**3**) 57 + 30; (**4**) 45 + 20.

4. Explain that students should write and solve problem 1 to the right of the first grid on one of their sheets. After they have found the sum, they are to verify their answer by coloring squares on the grid. They should color squares equaling the number of the first addend in one color, and then color the squares equaling the number of the second addend in another color. Counting the total amount of squares they colored should equal the sum they found. They are to do this for each problem.

CLOSURE

Check your students' answers and grids. Instruct your students to write an explanation briefly listing the steps to solve an addition problem.

ANSWERS

The colored squares on their grids should equal the sums of the problems. (**1**) 39 (**2**) 58 (**3**) 87 (**4**) 65

Number and Operations in Base Ten: 1.NBT.5

"Use place value understanding and properties of operations to add and subtract."

> 5. "Given a two-digit number, mentally find 10 more or 10 less than the number, without having to count; explain the reasoning used."

BACKGROUND

Being able to mentally add 10 to or subtract 10 from a given two-digit number requires that students have a sound understanding of addition and subtraction. They must also understand place value for tens and ones.

 ACTIVITY: THE GAME OF FINDING 10 MORE OR 10 LESS

Working in groups, students will play a game in which they must mentally find 10 more or 10 less than a given two-digit number. They receive 1 point for every correct answer. The student in each group with the most points at the end of the game is the winner.

MATERIALS

1 copy of reproducible, "10 More or 10 Less Cards," for each group; reproducible, "Score Sheet for 10 More or 10 Less," for each student; scissors or paper cutter for the teacher.

PREPARATION

Make enough copies of the reproducible "10 More or 10 Less Cards" so that each group will have a full set of cards. Cut out the cards from each reproducible, keeping the cards of each in separate piles and in order.

PROCEDURE

1. Hand out a separate set of cards, face down, to each group of students. Tell your students to keep the cards face down. Also hand out copies of "Score Sheet for 10 More or 10 Less" to each student.

2. Explain to your students that they will play a game in which they will be given a number on a card, and they will mentally have to add 10 to it or subtract 10 from it. They will receive 1 point for each correct answer.

3. Explain that the students in each group play against each other. The game starts when one student picks a card. He reads the card aloud, saying the problem number (problem number 1, for instance), and the problem (for example, 10 more than 50). All group members are to then find the answer mentally; they are not permitted to work the problem out on paper. They should write the answer to the problem on their score sheet next to the problem's number. Another student picks a card and the procedure continues.

4. Explain that they will tally their scores on their score sheets after everyone in the class has solved all the problems.

5. Start the game, which ends when all of the problems have been solved.

CLOSURE

Announce the answers to the problems so that your students can check that their answers on their score sheets are correct. They should give themselves 1 point for each correct answer and 0 points for an incorrect answer. After students tally their scores, announce the winners of each group. Review some of the problems and ask volunteers to explain the reasoning they used to solve the problems.

ANSWERS

(1) 60 **(2)** 33 **(3)** 87 **(4)** 18 **(5)** 81 **(6)** 25 **(7)** 62 **(8)** 29 **(9)** 73 **(10)** 76 **(11)** 68 **(12)** 59 **(13)** 24 **(14)** 37 **(15)** 70 **(16)** 45 **(17)** 74 **(18)** 61

1) 10 more than 50	2) 10 less than 43	3) 10 more than 77
4) 10 less than 28	5) 10 less than 91	6) 10 more than 15
7) 10 more than 52	8) 10 less than 39	9) 10 more than 63
10) 10 less than 86	11) 10 more than 58	12) 10 more than 49
13) 10 less than 34	14) 10 more than 27	15) 10 less than 80
16) 10 less than 55	17) 10 more than 64	18) 10 less than 71

Name_____

SCORE SHEET FOR 10 MORE OR 10 LESS

	Answer	Point		Answer	Point
1)	_____	_____	2)	_____	_____
3)	_____	_____	4)	_____	_____
5)	_____	_____	6)	_____	_____
7)	_____	_____	8)	_____	_____
9)	_____	_____	10)	_____	_____
11)	_____	_____	12)	_____	_____
13)	_____	_____	14)	_____	_____
15)	_____	_____	16)	_____	_____
17)	_____	_____	18)	_____	_____

Number and Operations in Base Ten: 1.NBT.6

"Use place value understanding and properties of operations to add and subtract."

6. "Subtract multiples of 10 in the range 10–90 from multiples of 10 in the range 10–90 (positive or zero differences), using concrete models or drawings and strategies based on place value, properties of operations, and/or the relationship between addition and subtraction; relate the strategy to a written method and explain the reasoning used."

BACKGROUND

Subtracting multiples of 10 between 10 and 90 helps students gain the skills necessary to subtract any two-digit number from any larger two-digit number. Using models to represent subtraction is an excellent way for students to see the relationships between the numbers in a subtraction problem.

 ACTIVITY: SOLVING AND MODELING SUBTRACTION PROBLEMS

Working in groups, students will solve subtraction problems using interlocking base ten blocks.

MATERIALS

100 interlocking base ten blocks for each group of students; reproducible, "Subtracting Multiples of 10," for each student.

PROCEDURE

1. Hand out the materials. Explain that students are to use the blocks to model and solve the subtraction problems on the reproducible. They will also write an explanation of the strategy they used to solve the problems on a separate sheet of paper.

2. Present this problem on the board as an example: 70 – 20. Ask your students how they could model and solve this problem using their base ten blocks. A student might answer that you could start with 7 groups of 10 blocks, which equals 70. Subtracting 20 means taking away 2 groups of 10, leaving 5 groups of ten, which equals 50.

3. Explain that although students are to work together using the base ten blocks to model each problem on the reproducible, they are to write the answers to the problems on their own copy of the reproducible. Then, on a separate sheet of paper, each student is also to write a description of the strategies or methods used to solve the problems.

Discuss the answers as a class. Ask volunteers to explain the strategies or reasoning they used to solve the problems.

ANSWERS

(**1**) 30 (**2**) 20 (**3**) 10 (**4**) 40 (**5**) 0 (**6**) 20 (**7**) 20 (**8**) 10 (**9**) 30

SUBTRACTING MULTIPLES OF 10

Directions: Subtract.

1) $\begin{array}{r} 60 \\ -30 \\ \hline \end{array}$	2) $\begin{array}{r} 80 \\ -60 \\ \hline \end{array}$	3) $\begin{array}{r} 30 \\ -20 \\ \hline \end{array}$
4) $\begin{array}{r} 90 \\ -50 \\ \hline \end{array}$	5) $\begin{array}{r} 10 \\ -10 \\ \hline \end{array}$	6) $\begin{array}{r} 50 \\ -30 \\ \hline \end{array}$
7) $\begin{array}{r} 40 \\ -20 \\ \hline \end{array}$	8) $\begin{array}{r} 20 \\ -10 \\ \hline \end{array}$	9) $\begin{array}{r} 70 \\ -40 \\ \hline \end{array}$

Measurement and Data: 1.MD.1

"Measure lengths indirectly and by iterating length units."

> 1. "Order three objects by length; compare the lengths of two objects indirectly by using a third object."

BACKGROUND

For young students, their first experiences with measurement are often indirect. For example, they may compare lengths by recognizing that one object is longer than another. Conversely, they may realize that an object is shorter than another. Experiences with indirect measurement help to prepare students for eventually using measurement tools.

ACTIVITY: ORDERING AND COMPARING OBJECTS BY LENGTH

Students will cut out and compare the lengths of three objects.

MATERIALS

Scissors; crayons; reproducible, "Lengths," for each student.

PROCEDURE

1. Hand out the materials. Explain that the reproducible contains three rectangles. All of the rectangles are equal in width but they have different lengths. A color is written on each one: blue, green, or red.

2. Explain that students are to color each rectangle according to the color written on it, and then cut out each rectangle.

3. After they have colored and cut out their rectangles, explain that they are to place the rectangles in order from longest to shortest.

4. Ask students questions, such as the following:

   - Which rectangle (blue, green, or red) is the longest?
   - Which is the shortest?
   - Which rectangle is longer than one rectangle but shorter than another rectangle?

Instruct your students to take a pencil or crayon and compare its length to the lengths of the three rectangles. Tell your students to place their pencils or crayons and rectangles in order from longest to shortest. Next, tell them to place their pencils or crayons and rectangles in order from shortest to longest. Ask your students: Why might the orders be different for different students?

Blue

Green

Red

Measurement and Data: 1.MD.2

"Measure lengths indirectly and by iterating length units."

---

2. "Express the length of an object as a whole number of length units, by laying multiple copies of a shorter object (the length unit) end to end; understand that the length measurement of an object is the number of same-size length units that span it with no gaps or overlaps. *Limit to contexts where the object being measured is spanned by a whole number of length units with no gaps or overlaps.*"

BACKGROUND

A length unit is a measurement that can be used to measure other lengths. Before young students begin working with standard measurement units, such as inches or feet, or centimeters or meters, they can use length units to find the length of an object.

ACTIVITY: MEASURING STRING IN LENGTH UNITS

Students will measure a piece of string using interlocking 2-centimeter unit cubes as a length unit.

MATERIALS

15 interlocking 2-centimeter unit cubes; transparent tape; 1 30-centimeter length of string per student. (Note: You can use interlocking cubes of other sizes for this activity; however, you must then adjust the length of string accordingly.)

PREPARATION

Cut string into 30 centimeter lengths so that each student will have one piece of string that is 30 centimeters long.

PROCEDURE

1. Hand out the materials. Instruct your students to tape the ends of their string to their desk so that the string is stretched out to its full length.

2. Explain that students are to find the length of the string, using the interlocking cubes as their length unit. The length unit serves as the unit of measurement. Emphasize that there can be no gaps or overlaps as they measure. Be sure your students understand what is meant by "gap" and "overlap." By interlocking the cubes, students will ensure that there are no gaps or overlaps.

3. Lead your students through the following exercises:

- If each cube is one length unit, how long is the string in length units? Give students time to investigate and find an answer. They should find that it is 15 length units long.

- Instruct your students to lock 3 cubes together. If the 3 cubes are now the length unit, how long is the string? Students should find that it is 5 length units long.

- Instruct your students to lock 5 cubes together. If the 5 cubes are now the length unit, how long is the string? They should find that it is 3 length units long.

CLOSURE

Discuss that the length of an object is the number of same-size length units that span it without gaps or overlaps. Ask your students: If the length unit changes, does the length of the object being measured change? Ask them to explain their answers.

Measurement and Data: 1.MD.3

"Tell and write time."

> 3. "Tell and write time in hours and half-hours using analog and digital clocks."

BACKGROUND

Telling and writing time are fundamental skills. Because most homes are more likely to have digital rather than analog clocks, most young children are more likely to be able to tell time on digital clocks than on analog clocks. Practice and periodic review can help students master telling and writing time with both types of clock.

ACTIVITY 1: A BOOK ABOUT TELLING TIME

The teacher reads and discusses the book *Telling Time: How to Tell Time on Digital and Analog Clocks!* by Jules Older.

MATERIAL

1 copy of *Telling Time: How to Tell Time on Digital and Analog Clocks!* by Jules Older (Charlesbridge, 2000).

PROCEDURE

1. Gather your students around you so that you can share with them the book's illustrations as you read. Explain that you will read a book about time to them.

2. Before you start reading, ask your students questions about time and their day, such as:
   - What time is it now?
   - What time did school start?
   - What time is lunch?
   - What time does school end?
   - What time do you wake up in the morning?
   - What time do you go to sleep at night?

3. As you read, pause and discuss the definitions of time words that are provided, for example, "seconds," "minutes," "hours," "weeks," "months," "years," "calendar," and so on. Have your students answer the time questions that are asked throughout the book.

CLOSURE

Review the time words. Discuss why it is important to tell time on both kinds of clocks. Tell students to pretend it is 4:00. Ask how they would show this on a digital clock and on an analog clock. Provide some other times and ask how these times would appear on both clocks.

ACTIVITY 2: PRACTICING TELLING TIME ON A WEB SITE

Using a Web site, the teacher leads an activity in which students answer time questions on virtual digital and analog clocks.

MATERIALS

1 dry-erase board; 1 dry-erase marker; 1 eraser or dry-erase cloth for each student; computer with Internet access; digital projector for the teacher.

PROCEDURE

1. Hand out the materials. Explain that the class will view clocks on a Web site and will answer questions about time.

2. Go to http://nlvm.usu.edu/. Click on "Pre-K–2," "Measurement," and then click on "Time—Analog and Digital Clocks." You will see an analog clock and a digital clock. Below the clocks are boxes for "Link Clocks," "Show current time," and "Show seconds." Directly below the digital clock are up/down arrows for changing hours, minutes, and seconds. Click on the X in the "Show seconds" box to remove the seconds from the digital clock. To change the time on the digital clock, move the up/down arrows for hours or minutes. To change the time on the analog clock, place the cursor on one of the hands and move it to the desired time. If you prefer to work with one clock at a time, remove the X by clicking on the box next to "Link Clocks."

3. Explain to your students that for the first part of this activity, you will show them times on the analog clock and that they are to tell what time it is. Start by removing the Xs from the boxes below the clocks. Tell your students that for now they are to ignore the digital clock. Move the hands on the analog clock to show times, for example, 3:00, 4:30, 9:00, and so on. After you present a time, ask for students to tell you what time it is. Present several different times.

4. Explain that for the next part of the activity, you will announce a time and students are to write the time on their dry-erase boards, just as if their boards were a digital clock. Ask your students to hold up their boards so that you can check their answers. Placing an X in "Link Clocks" will enable you to show your students the correct time on both clocks so that they can see the correct answers. Announce several different times, using hours and half-hours.

CLOSURE

Ask volunteers to suggest times for students to write on their dry-erase boards. Show the correct times on both clocks.

Measurement and Data: 1.MD.4

"Represent and interpret data."

4. "Organize, represent, and interpret data with up to three categories; ask and answer questions about the total number of data points, how many in each category, and how many more or less in one category than in another."

BACKGROUND

Being able to organize, represent, and interpret data are skills that extend far beyond math into every subject. These skills underscore the importance of math across the curriculum.

 ACTIVITY: WORKING WITH DATA

Working in pairs or groups of three, students will use spinners to generate data that they will organize, represent, and interpret.

MATERIALS

1 spinner with 3 colors; reproducible, "Spinner Data Sheet," for each pair or group of students; reproducible, "Spinner Data Questions," for each student.

PREPARATION

Because spinners from different companies often come in different colors, write in the colors of your spinners on the chart and for questions 3, 4, and 5 on the reproducible "Spinner Data Questions" before copying.

PROCEDURE

1. Hand out the materials. Explain that students will use their spinners to generate data that they will record on the reproducible "Spinner Data Sheet." After recording their data, they will organize and interpret the data by answering the questions on the reproducible "Spinner Data Questions."

2. Explain that students are to take turns spinning the spinner. After each spin, they should record the color on which the spinner landed on their data sheet. They are to complete 20 spins.

3. Explain that after they have completed 20 spins, each student is to answer the questions on their copy of the reproducible "Spinner Data Questions," based on the results of the spins. Note that if the spinner landed an equal number of times on two colors, students should not write an answer for "More" or "Less" for questions 3, 4, or 5, but instead complete the final sentence of the question. Likewise, if students write an answer for "More" or "Less," they should not write an answer for the final sentence of the question. (Note: Depending on your students, you may prefer to answer questions 3, 4, and 5 as a class.)

CLOSURE

Discuss students' results and the answers to the questions. Have students compare their results with the results of another pair or group. Ask your students why they think the data varied for different pairs and groups.

SPINNER DATA SHEET

Spin	Color	Spin	Color
1		11	
2		12	
3		13	
4		14	
5		15	
6		16	
7		17	
8		18	
9		19	
10		20	

Name_____

SPINNER DATA QUESTIONS

Directions: Answer the questions.

1. What was the total number of spins? _____

2. How many times did the spinner land on each color? Fill in the chart.

Color	Number

3. How many <u>more</u> or <u>less</u> times did the spinner land on _____

than on _____? _____ More _____ Less

The spinner landed _____ times on each color.

4. How many <u>more</u> or <u>less</u> times did the spinner land on _____

than on _____? _____ More _____ Less

The spinner landed _____ times on each color.

5. How many <u>more</u> or <u>less</u> times did the spinner land on _____

than on _____? _____ More _____ Less

The spinner landed _____ times on each color.

Geometry: 1.G.1

"Reason with shapes and their attributes."

1. "Distinguish between defining attributes (e.g., triangles are closed and three-sided) versus non-defining attributes (e.g., color, orientation, overall size); build and draw shapes to possess defining attributes."

BACKGROUND

A defining attribute is an attribute that helps to distinguish a shape from other shapes. For example, the defining attributes of a square are four congruent sides and four right angles. This clearly distinguishes a square from a triangle, which is a three-sided, closed figure. Non-defining attributes comprise attributes such as color (a blue square and a red square are still squares), size (a big triangle and a small triangle are still triangles, regardless of the lengths of their sides), or orientation (a rectangle orientated vertically and a rectangle orientated horizontally are still rectangles). For many students, understanding the difference between defining and non-defining attributes requires practice and review.

ACTIVITY 1: A BOOK ABOUT LINES AND SHAPES

The teacher reads and discusses the book *When a Line Bends . . . A Shape Begins* by Rhonda Gowler Greene to the class.

MATERIALS

1 copy of *When a Line Bends . . . A Shape Begins* by Rhonda Gowler Greene (Houghton Mifflin, 1997).

PROCEDURE

1. Have your students sit near you so that you can share the illustrations in the book with them.

2. As you read, discuss some of the shapes, especially lines, squares, rectangles, and triangles. Show the illustrations of the shapes and point out their defining attributes:

   - A square has 4 congruent sides and 4 right angles.

   - A rectangle has 4 sides. Its opposite sides are congruent, and it has 4 right angles.

   - A triangle has 3 sides and 3 angles.

- A circle is a closed curved line that surrounds a central point.
- As you discuss defining attributes, also discuss non-defining attributes, such as color, size, and orientation.

CLOSURE

Have volunteers point out examples of squares, rectangles, triangles, and circles in the classroom. Review the defining attributes of these shapes. Also review non-defining attributes.

ACTIVITY 2: DRAWING SHAPES

Students will use attribute blocks to build and draw a shape. They will label the defining attributes of the specific shapes that they used to build their new shape.

MATERIALS

A variety of attribute blocks; crayons; drawing paper for each student.

PROCEDURE

1. Hand out the materials. Write the words *square*, *rectangle*, *triangle*, and *circle* on the board. Ask your students to identify the defining attributes of each shape, for example: How can you tell a square from a rectangle? From a triangle? From a circle? (If your students are familiar with more shapes, such as trapezoids and pentagons, you might write these on the board as well and discuss their defining attributes.) You might also discuss non-defining attributes.

2. Explain that your students are to use their attribute blocks to build a new shape. Suggest some possible shapes they might build: a robot made with squares, rectangles, and a circle; a snowman or snowwoman made with circles; a car made with a rectangle, square, and circles. Brainstorm with your students to generate more ideas of shapes they can make with their attribute blocks.

3. Explain that after they have created their new shape, they are to draw it on their paper. Below the shape, they are to write the defining attributes of the shapes they used to make it. Instruct them to start their sentences with: "A square has . . .," "A rectangle has . . .," and so on. They should then color the new shape they made.

4. Have your students share their drawings with a classmate. Students should verify that the defining attributes that their partner wrote are correct.

ACTIVITY 3: VIRTUAL SHAPES AND ATTRIBUTES

Using a virtual geoboard at a Web site, the teacher will project various geometric shapes of different sizes, colors, and orientations. Students are to name the shapes and identify their defining attributes.

MATERIALS

Computer with Internet access; digital projector for the teacher.

PROCEDURE

1. Explain that shapes have different sizes and orientations. Review the names and examples of shapes, such as squares, rectangles, triangles, parallelograms, and trapezoids. (Note: You will not be able to make circles on the virtual geoboard.)

2. Ask volunteers to explain the difference between defining and non-defining attributes of shapes. For example: How can you tell a square is a square? What makes a square different from a triangle? What makes a square different from a rectangle? Are color, size, or a shape's position defining attributes? Students should realize that these are non-defining attributes.

3. Go to http://nlvm.usu.edu/. Click on "Pre-K–2," "Measurement," and then click on "Geoboard." Explain that you are going to make some shapes, and that students are to name the shapes and describe their defining attributes. The shapes will be in different sizes and orientations.

4. To create a shape, click on a virtual rubber band under "Bands," drag the band to the board, and place it on a peg. Clicking on the band again enables you to stretch it to other pegs to make various shapes, for example, squares, rectangles, triangles, trapezoids, hexagons, and so on, of various sizes and orientations. You can then take more bands and make more shapes on the same screen. Clicking on a band and then clicking on a color highlights a shape in that color. To delete a shape, click on the band to highlight it, and then click on the "Delete" button. Clicking on the "Clear" button will clear the entire screen.

5. Create several shapes and ask for volunteers to name the shapes. Have students identify the defining attributes of each shape.

Review the shapes you covered in this activity. Place one example of each on the geoboard at the same time. Ask students to name each one and describe its defining attributes.

Geometry: 1.G.2

"Reason with shapes and their attributes."

2. "Compose two-dimensional shapes (rectangles, squares, trapezoids, triangles, half-circles, and quarter-circles) or three-dimensional shapes (cubes, right rectangular prisms, right circular cones, and right circular cylinders) to create a composite shape, and compose new shapes from the composite shape."

BACKGROUND

Once students understand the difference between two-dimensional shapes and three-dimensional shapes, they are able to reason more accurately in geometric terms. Two-dimensional shapes lie in a plane. They have two dimensions such as length and width. A square drawn on a sheet of paper is a good example of a two-dimensional shape. A three-dimensional shape may be thought of as a solid that has length, width, and height. A die is an example.

ACTIVITY 1: MAKING TWO-DIMENSIONAL SHAPES

Students will form composite shapes from two or more basic, two-dimensional shapes. They will then use the composite shapes to form another shape.

MATERIALS

Scissors; glue stick; unlined paper; reproducible, "Using Shapes," for each student.

PROCEDURE

1. Explain that two-dimensional shapes lie flat in a plane and have two dimensions, such as length and width. Ask your students to provide some examples of two-dimensional shapes: a picture on a page of a book, a photograph, or the surface of a sheet of paper, for example.

2. Hand out the materials. Explain that the reproducible has two parts.

3. Tell your students to complete part 1 before they start part 2. For each part, they are to cut out the shapes, use them to form a composite shape, and then use the composite shape to form another shape. For part 1, this final shape is a square; for part 2, it is a circle. After they have formed the final shapes, they are to glue them on their paper.

ACTIVITY 2: MAKING A THREE-DIMENSIONAL SHAPE

Working in small groups, students will use interlocking cubes to create a composite three-dimensional shape and then use the composite shape to create another composite three-dimensional shape. They will describe their results.

MATERIALS

About 30 interlocking cubes for each group.

PROCEDURE

1. Review that a three-dimensional shape is a solid that has length, width, and height. It is different from a two-dimensional shape that lies in a plane and has only the dimensions of length and width. Ask your students to provide some examples of three-dimensional shapes such as a cabinet, a box, or a globe.

2. Distribute the interlocking cubes and point out that a cube is a three-dimensional shape. Explain that students are to use their cubes to create a composite shape consisting of at least two cubes and then use the composite shape to create a new three-dimensional shape.

3. Explain that they may create various composite shapes by connecting cubes. For example, if they were to use four cubes to make a composite shape, they could use several combinations of this composite shape (four cubes) to make another three-dimensional

shape. Obviously, they can create a variety of composite shapes, and the types of other three-dimensional shapes they may make are left to their imaginations.

CLOSURE

Have groups share and discuss their three-dimensional shapes with another group. Ask students to explain how they know the shapes they created are three-dimensional.

PART 1

Use these shapes to form two rectangles. Then use the rectangles to form a large square.

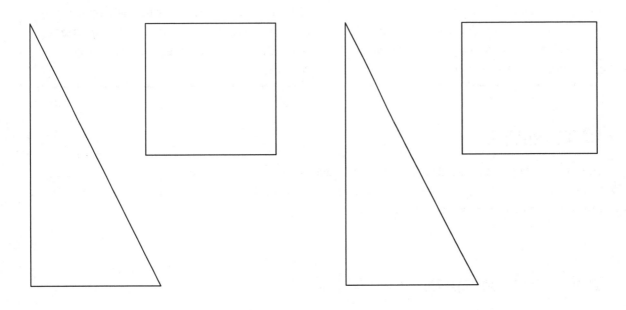

PART 2

Use these shapes to form two half-circles. Then use the half-circles to form a circle.

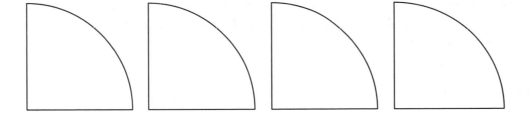

Geometry: 1.G.3

"Reason with shapes and their attributes."

3. "Partition circles and rectangles into two and four equal shares, describe the shares using the words *halves*, *fourths*, and *quarters*, and use the phrases *half of*, *fourth of*, and *quarter of*. Describe the whole as two of, or four of the shares. Understand for these examples that decomposing into more equal shares creates smaller shares."

BACKGROUND

In order to describe geometric figures, mathematical principles, and concepts, students must understand and be able to use the correct vocabulary. Terms such as *halves*, *fourths*, and *quarters* are necessary to describe partitions of figures.

ACTIVITY 1: PARTITIONING CIRCLES

Students will cut out a circle and divide it into halves and fourths. They will color each part according to the teacher's directions. Then they will turn the circle over and color specific parts with colors of their choice. They will describe the parts of the circle they colored.

MATERIALS

Scissors; one red, one blue, and one green crayon; three additional crayons of various colors other than red, blue, and green; reproducible, "Circle," for each student; 1 copy of the reproducible for the teacher.

PREPARATION

Cut out a circle from the reproducible so that you can use it to demonstrate what students are to do.

PROCEDURE

1. Explain that students will cut out a circle, divide it into halves and fourths, and color parts of the circle according to your instructions. To show your students the meaning of *halves* and *fourths*, sketch two circles on the board. Divide one into halves and the other into fourths.

2. Hand out the materials. Instruct your students to cut out the circle on the reproducible.

3. Explain that students are to divide their circle into halves. Demonstrate how they may divide the circle into halves by folding the top of the circle down to meet the bottom of the circle so that both parts align. Open the circle, showing that the crease divides the circle into two equal parts. Explain that each part is called a *half;* the two parts are called *halves*.

4. Next explain that students are to divide their circle into fourths. Show them how they can do this by first refolding the circle into halves so that the crease is on the top. Then fold the right-hand side of the circle over so that it aligns with the left-hand side of the circle as pictured below.

Circle   One-Half   One-Fourth

5. Tell your students to open their circle. Explain that it now has four equal parts, and that each part is *one-fourth,* or *one quarter,* of the circle.

6. Instruct your students to color one-half of their circle green; color one-fourth of their circle red; and color one-fourth of their circle blue. Check your students' work. Show examples of circles that are colored correctly, and explain that there are different ways to color the circles correctly, based on the directions you gave.

7. Instruct your students to turn their circles over so that the colored side is facing down. Tell them to choose three different crayons (perhaps purple, yellow, and brown). They are to choose one of these crayons and color one-half of the circle; use another crayon to color one-fourth of the circle; and use the third crayon to color the other quarter of the circle.

CLOSURE

Ask your students to describe the circle they colored using the terms *half, fourth,* and *quarter.* Ask them to describe how a *fourth* compares with a *half.*

ACTIVITY 2: PARTITIONING RECTANGLES

Students will cut out and divide a rectangle into halves and fourths. They will color each part of the rectangle according to the teacher's directions. Then they will turn the rectangle over and color specific parts with colors of their choice. They will describe the parts of the rectangle they colored.

Scissors; one red, one blue, and one green crayon; three additional crayons of various colors other than red, blue, and green; reproducible, "Rectangle," for each student; 1 copy of the reproducible for the teacher.

PREPARATION

Cut out a rectangle from the reproducible so that you can use it to demonstrate what students are to do.

PROCEDURE

1. Explain that students will cut out a rectangle, divide it into halves and fourths, and color parts of the rectangle according to your instructions.

2. Hand out the materials and tell your students to cut out the rectangle on the reproducible.

3. Explain that they are to divide the rectangle into halves. Demonstrate how they may do this: Hold the rectangle lengthwise and fold the top of it down to meet its bottom so that both parts align. Open the rectangle, showing that the crease divides the rectangle into two equal parts, called halves. Each part is one-half of the rectangle.

4. Show your students how to divide the rectangle into fourths. Refold the rectangle into halves so that the crease is on top. Then fold the right-hand side of the rectangle over so that it aligns with the left-hand side of the rectangle as shown below.

Rectangle   One-Half   One-Fourth

5. Tell your students to open their rectangle. Explain that it now has four equal parts. Each part is one-fourth, or one quarter, of the rectangle. Explain that two of these equal parts make up one half of the rectangle.

6. Instruct your students to color one-half of their rectangle green; color one-fourth of their rectangle red; and color one-fourth of their rectangle blue. Check your students' work. Show examples of rectangles that are colored correctly, and explain that there are different ways to color the rectangles, based on your directions.

7. Now ask your students to turn their rectangle over so that the colored side is facing down. Tell them to choose three different crayons (perhaps purple, yellow, and brown). They are to choose one of these crayons and color half of the rectangle; use another crayon to color one-fourth of the rectangle; and use the third crayon to color the other quarter of the rectangle.

CLOSURE

Ask your students to describe the rectangle they colored using the terms: *half, fourth,* and *quarter*. Ask them to describe how the *fourth* compares with the *half*.

Standards and Activities for Grade 2

Operations and Algebraic Thinking: 2.OA.1

"Represent and solve problems involving addition and subtraction."

1. "Use addition and subtraction within 100 to solve one- and two-step word problems involving situations of adding to, taking from, putting together, taking apart, and comparing, with unknowns in all positions, e.g., by using drawings and equations with a symbol for the unknown number to represent the problem."

BACKGROUND

Presenting students with various addition and subtraction word problems broadens their understanding of these basic operations. While one-step word problems present students with rather straightforward situations, two-step problems require more careful analysis of data. To solve any word problem, encourage your students to do the following:

1. Read the problem carefully. Reread it if necessary.

2. Decide what the problem is asking.

3. Decide which operation, or operations, can be used to solve the problem.

4. Do the required computation.

5. Double-check your work.

6. Ask yourself if the answer makes sense.

 ## ACTIVITY 1: WORD PROBLEMS INVOLVING ADDING TO AND TAKING FROM

Working in pairs or groups of three, students will write equations and solve addition and subtraction word problems within 100 that involve situations of adding to and taking from. Then, working individually, they will represent two of the problems on a 100-unit grid.

MATERIALS

Crayons; reproducibles, "Word Problems (Adding To and Taking From)" and "Grids for Showing Addition and Subtraction," for each student.

PROCEDURE

1. Discuss the steps for solving word problems as noted in the Background.

2. Hand out the materials. Explain that the reproducible "Word Problems (Adding To and Taking From)" has six word problems students must solve. Depending on your class, you might find it helpful to read the problems together. You may want to point out that problems 5 and 6 are two-step problems. The reproducible "Grids for Showing Addition and Subtraction" has two 100-unit grids that students are to use to represent two of the problems.

3. Explain that students are to work with their partner, or partners. They are to discuss, write an equation with a symbol for an unknown number, and then solve each problem. After solving all of the problems, students are to work individually, choosing two problems and representing the problems on their grids. (Note: You may prefer that your students work together on this part of the activity as well.)

- For the first grid, explain that they are to choose either problem 1, 2, 3, or 4. For the second grid, they are to choose problem 5 or 6. They are to circle the number of each problem they choose.

- Explain that for each grid students are to use crayons to color squares to represent the problem they chose. For example, to represent $25 + 54$, students might color 25 squares (two columns of 10 and 5 squares in a third column) blue and then color 54 more squares (five columns of 10 and 4 more squares) green to show a total of 79 squares. The total number of the colored squares, 79, is the sum of $25 + 54$. To represent $63 - 21$, students might lightly color 63 squares in yellow and then color 21 of those squares darkly with red, leaving 42 squares. The total number of the squares that remain yellow, 42, is the difference of $63 - 21$.

- Point out that at "Work Space" students are to show the math that they used to solve the problem.

- Explain that under each grid students are to write two equations. The first equation should contain a symbol for an unknown number, $25 + 54 = ?$, for example. The second equation should be written with the solution, $25 + 54 = 79$. (Note: Depending on the problem, the position of the unknown symbol may change.)

CLOSURE

Discuss the equations and answers to the problems. Also discuss how the problems represent situations of adding to and taking from. Have volunteers share their grids with the class. Display students' grids.

ANSWERS

Grids should reflect the following answers. Equations may vary. An equation is provided for each problem. **(1)** $68 - ? = 42$; 26 **(2)** $22 + 38 = ?$; 60 **(3)** $? + 35 = 62$; 27 **(4)** $? - 34 = 25$; 59 **(5)** $84 - 51 - 20 = ?$; 13 **(6)** $23 + 21 + 19 = ?$; 63

ACTIVITY 2: WORD PROBLEMS INVOLVING PUTTING TOGETHER, TAKING APART, AND COMPARING

Working in pairs or groups of three, students will write equations and solve addition and subtraction word problems within 100 that involve situations of putting together, taking apart, and comparing. Then, working individually, they will represent two of the problems on a 100-unit grid.

MATERIALS

Crayons; reproducibles, "Word Problems (Putting Together, Taking Apart, and Comparing)" and "Grids for Showing Addition and Subtraction," for each student.

PROCEDURE

1. Hand out the materials. Explain that the reproducible "Word Problems (Putting Together, Taking Apart, and Comparing)" has six word problems students must solve. Depending on your class, you might find it helpful to read the problems together. You may want to point out that problems 5 and 6 are two-step problems. The reproducible "Grids for Showing Addition and Subtraction" has two 100-unit grids that students are to use to represent two of the problems.

2. Explain that students are to work with their partner, or partners, to discuss, write an equation with a symbol for an unknown number, and solve each word problem. After solving the problems, they are to work individually, choosing two problems and representing the problems on their grids. (Note: You may prefer that your students also work together on this part of the activity.)

   - For the first grid, explain that they are to choose either problem 1, 2, 3, or 4. For the second grid, they are to choose problem 5 or 6. They should circle the number of each problem they choose.

   - For each grid, explain that students are to use crayons to color squares to represent the problem they chose. For example, to represent $45 + 22$, students might color 45 squares (four columns of 10 and 5 squares in a fifth column) blue and then color 22 more squares (two columns of 10 and 2 more squares) green to show a total of 67 squares. The total number of the colored squares, 67, is the sum. To represent $53 - 21$, students might lightly color 53 squares in yellow and then color 21 of those squares darkly with red, leaving 32 squares. The total number of the squares that remain yellow, 32, is the difference.

   - Explain that at "Work Space" students are to show the math that they used to solve the problem.

   - Explain that under each grid they are to write two equations. The first equation should contain a symbol for an unknown number, $45 + 22 = ?$, for example. The second equation should be written with the solution, $45 + 22 = 67$. (Note: Depending on the problem, the position of the unknown symbol may change.)

CLOSURE

Discuss the equations and answers to the problems. Also discuss how the problems show situations of putting together, taking apart, and comparing. Have volunteers share their grids with the class. Display students' grids.

ANSWERS

Grids should reflect the following answers. Equations may vary. An equation is provided for each problem. (**1**) $36 + 23 = ?; 59$ (**2**) $40 - 25 = ?; 15$ (**3**) $27 + 29 = ?; 56$ (**4**) $68 - 36 = ?; 32$ (**5**) $45 + 16 + 23 = ?; 84$ (**6**) $70 - 24 - 21 = ?; 25$

WORD PROBLEMS (ADDING TO AND TAKING FROM)

Directions: Write an equation with a symbol for the unknown number. Then solve each problem.

1. 68 students were on the playground. Some students were called to line up to go to class. 42 students were still on the playground. How many students left the playground to go to class?

2. 22 cars were parked in a lot. 38 more cars came and parked in the lot. How many cars were then parked in the lot?

3. Some students waited in line to enter the school in the morning. 35 more students came. A total of 62 students was now waiting in line. How many students were waiting in line before?

4. Some students were waiting for their buses after school. A bus came and picked up 34 students. 25 students were still waiting. How many students were waiting for the bus before?

5. The bakery had 84 free cookies on a table. Customers took 51 of the free cookies in the morning. They took 20 more free cookies in the afternoon. How many cookies were left?

6. Mrs. Rose's class, Mr. Smith's class, and Ms. Martino's class are going to the science fair. Mrs. Rose has 23 students. Mr. Smith has 21 students. Ms. Martino has 19 students. How many students are going to the science fair?

Name _____

WORD PROBLEMS (PUTTING TOGETHER, TAKING APART, AND COMPARING)

Directions: Write an equation with a symbol for the unknown number. Then solve each problem.

1. Jason has 23 fewer video games than Annie. Jason has 36 games. How many video games does Annie have?

2. Emma has 25 minutes of homework. Louis has 40 minutes of homework. How many more minutes of homework does Louis have than Emma?

3. Grandma's garden has 27 red flowers and 29 white flowers. How many flowers are in her garden?

4. 68 people were waiting in line at the theater. 36 were adults. The rest were children. How many were children?

5. 45 sheets of blue paper, 16 sheets of red paper, and 23 sheets of green paper were on the table. How many sheets of paper were on the table?

6. 70 students were at the book fair. 24 students were in Mr. Wilson's class. 21 students were in Ms. Jackson's class. The rest of the students were in Mrs. Garcia's class. How many students were in Mrs. Garcia's class?

Name _____

GRIDS FOR SHOWING ADDITION AND SUBTRACTION

Circle the number of your problem: 1, 2, 3, or 4.

Work Space

Equations: _____

Circle the number of your problem: 5 or 6.

Work Space

Equations: _____

Operations and Algebraic Thinking: 2.OA.2

"Add and subtract within 20."

> 2. "Fluently add and subtract within 20 using mental strategies. By end of Grade 2, know from memory all sums of two one-digit numbers."

BACKGROUND

As students master basic addition and subtraction skills, they should be able to mentally add and subtract within 20. Such fluency is a solid foundation for adding and subtracting larger numbers.

 ## ACTIVITY: MENTAL MATH GAME FOR ADDING AND SUBTRACTING WITHIN 20

Working in pairs or groups of three or four, students will play a game in which they mentally add and subtract within 20. Players receive 1 point for every correct answer. The student of each group who has the most points at the end of the game is the winner.

MATERIALS

1 copy of reproducible, "Mental Math Game Cards," for each group of students; "Mental Math Game Score Sheet" for each student; scissors or paper cutter for the teacher.

PREPARATION

Make enough copies of the reproducible "Mental Math Game Cards" so that each group will have a full set of cards. Cut out a set of cards for each group, keeping the cards for each group in a separate pile and in reverse order. Make enough copies of the reproducible "Mental Math Game Score Sheet" so that each student has his or her own sheet. (Note: Each reproducible contains two score sheets.) Cut the score sheets out.

PROCEDURE

1. Explain that students will play a game in their groups in which they are to mentally add or subtract numbers within 20. They may not use pencil and paper to work out the problems; however, they may use various strategies to solve the problems mentally. For example, they may use counting on, making ten, decomposing numbers, using the relationship between addition and subtraction, or creating equivalent sums.

2. Hand out a separate set of problem cards, face down, to each group of students. Tell your students to keep the cards face down. Note: Problem cards should be in order from 1 to 24 with problem number 1 on the top so that the first face-down card students pick will be problem 1. Next hand out the score sheets, one to each student. Students are to write their answers to the problems on their score sheets.

3. Explain that the students in each group play against each other. The game starts when one student picks a card. The card contains a problem and the answer to the problem. Because the card has both the problem and the answer, the student who picked the card does not solve this problem and leaves this answer space blank on her score sheet. She acts as the announcer and presents the problem number and problem to the other members of the group. The other group members then mentally find the answer to the problem. They should write the answer to the problem on their score sheet next to the problem's number. After all players in the group write their answers on their answer sheets, the announcer tells the group members the answer and the other students mark their answer right or wrong. Another student of the group now assumes the role of announcer and picks the next problem card. He announces the problem number and problem and the game continues.

4. Caution your students that as they pick a card, they should be careful not to reveal its answer. Announcers should speak slowly and clearly when presenting the problems. They may repeat the problem, if necessary.

5. Begin the game, which ends when all the cards have been picked.

CLOSURE

Provide the answers to the problems once more so that students can double-check that they marked their score sheets correctly. Have students tally their scores—1 point for each correct answer and no points for incorrect answers—and write the total after "Points" on their score sheets. Announce the winners in each group. Review some of the problems and ask volunteers to explain the reasoning they used to solve them.

1) $7 + 3$ Answer: 10	2) $15 - 9$ Answer: 6	3) $10 + 7$ Answer: 17	4) $4 + 11$ Answer: 15
5) $20 - 8$ Answer: 12	6) $13 - 5$ Answer: 8	7) $9 + 9$ Answer: 18	8) $6 - 0$ Answer: 6
9) $7 + 2$ Answer: 9	10) $19 - 8$ Answer: 11	11) $8 - 4$ Answer: 4	12) $7 + 13$ Answer: 20
13) $16 - 6$ Answer: 10	14) $9 - 9$ Answer: 0	15) $0 + 14$ Answer: 14	16) $8 + 11$ Answer: 19
17) $6 + 7$ Answer: 13	18) $10 - 8$ Answer: 2	19) $17 - 13$ Answer: 4	20) $15 - 8$ Answer: 7
21) $2 + 3$ Answer: 5	22) $14 - 6$ Answer: 8	23) $6 + 6$ Answer: 12	24) $12 + 4$ Answer: 16

MENTAL MATH GAME SCORE SHEET

Name _____   **Points:** _____

Directions: Write the answer to each problem next to its number.

1) _____   2) _____   3) _____   4) _____   5) _____   6) _____

7) _____   8) _____   9) _____   10) _____   11) _____   12) _____

13) _____   14) _____   15) _____   16) _____   17) _____   18) _____

19) _____   20) _____   21) _____   22) _____   23) _____   24) _____

- -

MENTAL MATH GAME SCORE SHEET

Name _____   **Points:** _____

Directions: Write the answer to each problem next to its number.

1) _____   2) _____   3) _____   4) _____   5) _____   6) _____

7) _____   8) _____   9) _____   10) _____   11) _____   12) _____

13) _____   14) _____   15) _____   16) _____   17) _____   18) _____

19) _____   20) _____   21) _____   22) _____   23) _____   24) _____

Operations and Algebraic Thinking: 2.OA.3

"Work with equal groups of objects to gain foundations for multiplication."

3. "Determine whether a group of objects (up to 20) has an odd or even number of members, e.g., by pairing objects or counting them by 2s; write an equation to express an even number as a sum of two equal addends."

BACKGROUND

Recognizing odd and even numbers is a basic concept underlying number sense. The number 2, for example, is a factor of all even numbers, but 2 is never a factor of an odd number. Building fundamental number sense is an important, yet often overlooked, exercise in early math learning.

ACTIVITY 1: A BOOK ABOUT AN EVEN-NUMBERED DAY

The teacher reads the book *My Even Day* to the class, using the ideas in the book to discuss even and odd numbers.

MATERIALS

My Even Day by Doris Fisher and Dani Sneed (Sylvan Dell Publishing, 2007).

PROCEDURE

1. Have your students sit so that you will be able to show illustrations in the book to them as you read. Explain that you are going to read a book about a boy who had an "even-numbered" day, when everything could be described by an even number.

2. As you read, pause periodically and share the illustrations with your students. Encourage them to find the hidden items that are in many of the illustrations. Most of the items, of course, illustrate even numbers.

3. Present the activities in the "For Creative Minds" section at the end of the book, which expands the concepts in the story.

CLOSURE

Ask your students to name a variety of even and odd numbers. Ask them to name things that show even and odd numbers. For example, a rectangle has four sides; a tricycle has three wheels.

ACTIVITY 2: SPILLING OBJECTS

Working in pairs or groups of three, students will spill up to 20 counters from a plastic cup and determine if the number of objects is even or odd. They will write an equation expressing every even number as a sum of two equal addends.

MATERIALS

20 counters; 1 plastic cup (or similar container); reproducible, "Even or Odd Numbers Recording Sheet," for each pair or group of students.

PROCEDURE

1. Hand out the materials. Explain that students are to use the counters to find even and odd numbers. They will write their findings on their recording sheet. If necessary, review some examples of even and odd numbers.

2. Explain the activity. Students are to place all of the counters in their cups. They are to spill some of the counters out across their desk or table. Then they are to count the counters, or pair them and count them by twos to determine if the number of counters is an even or odd number. After they have decided if the number is even or odd, they are to record the number on their recording sheet and write whether it is even or odd. For even numbers, they are to write an equation expressing the number as a sum of two equal addends. If a number is odd, students do not write an equation and should leave the equation space blank.

3. Provide this example. Tell your students to imagine that they spilled all 20 counters from their cup. They should write 20 in the space on their recording sheet under "Number." Because 20 is an even number, they should write the word "Even" under "Even or Odd." Under "Equations for Even Numbers" they should write $10 + 10 = 20$, showing that 20 can be expressed as two equal addends, 10 and 10. Remind your students that they would leave this space blank if a number is odd.

4. Explain that students are to complete the recording sheet. If they spill counters that result in a previous number, they should put all the counters back into the cup and try again.

CLOSURE

Discuss students' results. Have your students share some even numbers they tossed and the equations they wrote for them. Ask your students how they know whether a number is even or odd. Ask them to explain why odd numbers do not have two equal addends.

Names_____

EVEN OR ODD NUMBERS RECORDING SHEET

Directions: Complete the table.

Number	Even or Odd	Equations for Even Numbers

Operations and Algebraic Thinking: 2.OA.4

"Work with equal groups of objects to gain foundations for multiplication."

> 4. "Use addition to find the total number of objects arranged in rectangular arrays with up to 5 rows and up to 5 columns; write an equation to express the total as a sum of addends."

BACKGROUND

Rectangular arrays provide excellent models that show the relationship between addition and multiplication with whole numbers. By expressing arrays as a sum of addends, repeated addition can be linked to multiplication.

ACTIVITY: RECTANGULAR ARRAYS AND EQUATIONS

Working in pairs or groups of three, students will use spinners with numbers 1 to 5 to find the number of rows and columns of rectangular arrays. Students will use counters to create the arrays, and then draw representations of the arrays and write an equation that represents each array.

MATERIALS

1 spinner with numbers 1 to 5 (two sets of cards, each set numbered 1 to 5, may be substituted); 25 counters; crayons; 1 sheet of unlined paper for each pair or group of students. (Note: Although spinners are available from many school supply companies, you may prefer to make spinners of your own. Instructions can be found online. A phrase such as "making a spinner for the classroom" will result in helpful Web sites.)

PROCEDURE

1. Explain that a rectangular array is an arrangement of objects in rows and columns. An array might have 3 rows and 2 columns, 4 rows and 5 columns, 5 rows and 5 columns, and so on. Provide an example of an array on the board.

2. Explain that an array can be expressed as an equation showing the sum of objects as equal addends. For example, the total numbers of objects in an array of 3 rows and 4 columns can be expressed as $4 + 4 + 4 = 12$ or $3 \times 4 = 12$.

3. Hand out the materials. Explain that students are to use their spinners to find the number of rows and columns in rectangular arrays. Remind your students that rows are horizontal

and columns are vertical. They are to spin twice for each array. The first number they spin represents the number of rows in the array, and the second number they spin represents the number of columns. For example, if the first spin lands on 3, and the second spin lands on 5, students are to create an array that has 3 rows and 5 columns.

4. Explain that after they have found the number of rows and columns in an array, they are to create a model of the array using counters. An array with 3 rows and 5 columns, for example, should have 3 rows with each row containing 5 counters. After creating their arrays with counters, students are to draw their arrays on unlined paper, drawing small circles in place of counters. If you wish, suggest that your students color their arrays. Finally, under each array they draw, students are to write an equation that expresses the total number of objects as a sum of equal addends.

5. Instruct your students to create 5 arrays, using their spinners. They should identify the arrays they created that have the most and least counters.

CLOSURE

Check your students' arrays. Ask for volunteers to share their arrays and equations with the class. Find the array that was the largest. Find the smallest.

Depending on the abilities of your class, you may also want to make comparisons between arrays. For example, why do some different arrays have the same total number of counters? A 2 by 3 array and a 3 by 2 array both will contain 6 counters. This discussion will preview commutativity, which is an important skill in addition and multiplication.

Number and Operations in Base Ten: 2.NBT.1

"Understand place value."

> 1. "Understand that the three digits of a three-digit number represent amounts of hundreds, tens, and ones; e.g., 706 equals 7 hundreds, 0 tens, and 6 ones. Understand the following as special cases:
>
> **a.** "100 can be thought of as a bundle of tens—called a 'hundred.'
>
> **b.** "The numbers 100, 200, 300, 400, 500, 600, 700, 800, 900 refer to one, two, three, four, five, six, seven, eight, or nine hundreds (and 0 tens and 0 ones)."

BACKGROUND

Place value is the value of each digit in a number, based on the position of the digit. As students gain a greater understanding of place value, they gain a greater understanding of numbers in general and are able to perform operations with larger numbers.

 ACTIVITY 1: CREATING NUMBERS OF UP TO THREE DIGITS

Working in groups, students will use spinners with the numbers 0 to 9 to create numbers of up to three digits. They will represent the numbers with base ten blocks and record their results.

MATERIALS

Spinners with the numbers 0 to 9; base ten blocks (with 9 flats, 9 rods, and 9 units); crayons; unlined paper for each group of students.

PROCEDURE

1. Review that the digits in a three-digit number represent hundreds, tens, and ones. For example, the number 652 contains 6 hundreds, 5 tens, and 2 ones. Provide more examples, if necessary.

2. Hand out the materials. Explain that students are to use the spinners to create at least three numbers of up to three digits. The first number the spinner lands on represents the hundreds, the second number the spinner lands on represents the tens, and the third number the spinner lands on represents the ones. If, for example, three spins result in 3, 0, and 8, the number is 308. If the first spin lands on 0, there will be no hundreds in the number. If the first two spins land on 0, there will be no hundreds and no tens. If all three spins land on 0, students should spin again to try to find a three-digit number.

3. Explain that after students have created a number using their spinners, they are to represent the number using base ten blocks. They are then to record their results on unlined paper with a drawing and write the number under its drawing. (Note: Students need not draw 100 individual units to represent each flat or 10 individual units to represent each rod. Rather they may draw flats and rods and simply label them as 100 or 10.)

CLOSURE

Have each group of students exchange their drawings with the drawings of another group. Students should check and verify each other's work for accuracy. For example, if a group believes that any drawing they received is inaccurate, they should use their base ten blocks to check the representation of the number. Ask volunteers to summarize place value by noting the positions of hundreds, tens, and ones in three-digit numbers.

ACTIVITY 2: PLACE VALUE IN CYBERSPACE

The teacher leads an activity on a Web site that shows place value for three-digit numbers.

MATERIALS

Computer with Internet access; digital projector for the teacher.

PROCEDURE

1. Explain that you will visit a Web site that provides an activity on place value.

2. Go to http://nlvm.usu.edu/ and click on "Pre-K–2," "Number and Operations," and then click on "Base Blocks." The screen will show four columns. At the lower right, make sure that "Dec. Places" = 0, "Base" = 10, and "Columns" = 3. Make any changes that are necessary by clicking on the up/down buttons. The three columns represent hundreds, tens, and ones. Above each column is a virtual base ten block that represents the column's value; clicking on a block places a copy of it in its column. For example, to represent the number 125, click once on the block above the hundreds column, click twice on the block above the tens column, and click five times on the block above the ones column. After a block appears, you can click on it and drag it anywhere within the column. You can also arrange the blocks however you wish; you can even stack blocks upon each other. To delete a block, drag it to the trash can at the lower right of the screen. Clicking on "Clear" clears any work you may have done. Clicking on "Show a Problem" results in a number appearing at the top right.

3. Explain to your students the value of each column and place blocks in the columns for examples. As you place blocks, the value of the blocks appears at the right.

4. Next, click on "Show a Problem." A number will appear at the right. Ask your students how many blocks are needed in each column to represent the value of the number. Move the blocks your students suggest until the virtual base ten blocks represent the number. Do several problems to reinforce place value for your students.

CLOSURE

While still working at the Web site, ask your students to name a number and then to tell you how many blocks to place in each column to represent the number. Place the blocks to represent the problem and verify the students' answers.

Number and Operations in Base Ten: 2.NBT.2

"Understand place value."

> 2. "Count within 1,000; skip count by 5s, 10s, and 100s."

BACKGROUND

Counting within 1,000—especially when skip counting by 5s, 10s, and 100s—reinforces the understanding of place value. Once students are able to count fluently within 1,000, they can easily transfer this understanding to count within 2,000, 3,000, and so on.

 ACTIVITY: THE COUNTING GAME

Working in pairs or groups of three or four, students will play a game in which they must count within 1,000 by 1s, 5s, 10s, and 100s. They will receive 1 point for each correct answer. The student in each group who has the most points at the end of the game is the winner.

MATERIALS

Reproducible, "Counting Game Cards," for each pair or group of students; reproducible, "Counting Game Answer Sheet," for each student; scissors or paper cutter for the teacher.

PREPARATION

Make enough copies of "Counting Game Cards" for each pair or group of students. Cut out the cards and keep each set in reverse order in a separate pile.

PROCEDURE

1. Explain to your students that they will play a game in which they will count within 1,000 by 1s, 5s, 10s, and 100s.

2. Hand out to each group of students a separate set of game cards, face down, in order with problem card number 1 on top. Tell your students to keep the cards face down. Next, hand out the answer sheets, one to each student.

3. Explain that the students in each group play against each other. The game starts when one student picks a card. The cards contain problems that require students to count the next five numbers from a given number by 1s, 5s, 10s, or 100s, depending on the directions on each card. The cards also contain the answer to the problem, which is why the cards must

be kept face down. The student who picks a card reads the card number and the problem to the other students in her group, who then write the answer on their answer sheets. Point out to students that all five numbers in the answer should be written on one line. The student presenting the problem does not solve this problem and leaves this answer space blank on her answer sheet. Emphasize that students are to work individually and silently as they write their answers.

4. Explain that after the group members have written their answers, the student who picked the card says the answers, and the other group members correct their answers. Students receive 1 point for each problem if all five numbers are correct. Another student then picks a card and the game continues in the same manner. At the end of the game, students should tally their points and write the total in the space at the bottom of the sheet.

CLOSURE

Announce the students in each group with the highest scores as the winners. Discuss any numbers that students had difficulty counting. Present random numbers and have students say the next five numbers, counting either by 1s, 5s, 10s, or 100s.

COUNTING GAME CARDS

1) Count by 1s. What are the next 5 numbers after 608? Answer: 609, 610, 611, 612, 613	2) Count by 5s. What are the next 5 numbers after 225? Answer: 230, 235, 240, 245, 250	3) Count by 100s. What are the next 5 numbers after 300? Answer: 400, 500, 600, 700, 800
4) Count by 10s. What are the next 5 numbers after 510? Answer: 520, 530, 540, 550, 560	5) Count by 1s. What are the next 5 numbers after 756? Answer: 757, 758, 759, 760, 761	6) Count by 10s. What are the next 5 numbers after 870? Answer: 880, 890, 900, 910, 920
7) Count by 5s. What are the next 5 numbers after 85? Answer: 90, 95, 100, 105, 110	8) Count by 100s. What are the next 5 numbers after 500? Answer: 600, 700, 800, 900, 1,000	9) Count by 1s. What are the next 5 numbers after 328? Answer: 329, 330, 331, 332, 333
10) Count by 10s. What are the next 5 numbers after 460? Answer: 470, 480, 490, 500, 510	11) Count by 5s. What are the next 5 numbers after 345? Answer: 350, 355, 360, 365, 370	12) Count by 100s. What are the next 5 numbers after 100? Answer: 200, 300, 400, 500, 600

COUNTING GAME ANSWER SHEET

Directions: Write the answer for each "counting" game card next to its number.

1) _____

2) _____

3) _____

4) _____

5) _____

6) _____

7) _____

8) _____

9) _____

10) _____

11) _____

12) _____

Points: _____

Number and Operations in Base Ten: 2.NBT.3

"Understand place value."

> 3. "Read and write numbers to 1,000 using base-ten numerals, number names, and expanded form."

BACKGROUND

As students advance through the second grade math curriculum, they increasingly work with numbers within 1,000. They must be able to not only read and write these numbers using numerals, but also understand number names and expanded form. The expanded form of a number is directly related to place value. For example, written in expanded form, 735 is $700 + 30 + 5$. The expanded form clearly shows 7 hundreds, 3 tens, and 5 ones.

 ACTIVITY: PUZZLES AND EXPANDING NUMBERS

Working in pairs or groups of three, students will cut out cards containing parts of numbers, number names, and the expanded forms of numbers. They will put the pieces together to show two numbers, their word names, and their expanded forms.

MATERIALS

Scissors; glue stick; 1 sheet of construction paper; reproducible, "Expanded Number Puzzle Pieces," for each pair or group of students.

PROCEDURE

1. Present some numbers in word form, number form, and then expanded form on the board and discuss them. Following are some examples:

    - three hundred sixty-seven: $367 = 300 + 60 + 7$

    - six hundred four: $604 = 600 + 4$

    - two hundred twenty: $220 = 200 + 20$

2. Emphasize how the expanded form of a number is related to place value. For example, $367 = 300 + 60 + 7 = 3$ hundreds $+ 6$ tens $+ 7$ ones.

3. Hand out the materials. Explain that the reproducible contains numbers and words that students are to cut out and assemble to form two numbers, their word names, and expanded forms.

4. Explain that the puzzle pieces can be assembled into several different numbers. To make sure that students find the correct two numbers, write the following clues on the board:

- Each number has three digits.

- In one number, the tens digit is 5. This is one more than the hundreds digit and three less than the ones digit.

5. Tell your students that after they have figured out the answers, the numbers in word form, number form, and expanded form, they are to glue the pieces on their construction paper in a manner similar to the examples shown in procedure 1.

CLOSURE

Check your students' work. The assembled pieces of the puzzles follow:

- four hundred fifty-eight: $458 = 400 + 50 + 8$

- nine hundred twenty-six: $926 = 900 + 20 + 6$

Ask your students to relate the expanded forms of these numbers to place value.

9	four	8	hundred
eight	900 +	2	20 +
400 +	nine	50 +	6
5	twenty-	hundred	6
4	six	8	fifty-

Number and Operations in Base Ten: 2.NBT.4

"Understand place value."

4. "Compare two three-digit numbers based on meanings of the hundreds, tens, and ones digits, using >, =, and < symbols to record the results of the comparisons."

BACKGROUND

As students work with larger numbers, they must learn the number names and be able to write the numbers, and they must also understand the values of the numbers based on place value. To make comparisons, they should recognize and use the symbols > (greater than), = (equal), and < (less than).

 ACTIVITY: COMPARING NUMBERS THROUGH 999

Working in pairs or groups of three, students will use 10-sided dice to create numbers that they will compare using the symbols >, =, or <. They will record their results.

MATERIALS

1 10-sided die with the numbers 0 to 9 (a spinner with the numbers 0 to 9 can be substituted); reproducible, "Three-Digit Numbers Comparison Sheet," for each student.

PROCEDURE

1. Review the symbols >, =, and < by providing a few examples on the board, such as the following:

   - 732 > 694: 732 is greater than 694.

   - 405 = 405: 405 is equal to 405.

   - 916 < 918: 916 is less than 918.

2. Explain that students should compare the numbers according to place value. For example, 916 is less than 918 because although each number has 9 hundreds and 1 ten, 918 has 8 ones and 916 has 6 ones, which is 2 ones less.

3. Hand out the materials. Explain that students are to throw their die three times to make a number of up to three digits. The first throw represents the hundreds, the second throw

represents the tens, and the third throw represents the ones. Zeroes are included; therefore, students may end up with a three-digit number such as 309 or 200; a two-digit number if the first throw of the die results in 0, for example, 89; or if the first two throws of the die both result in 0, a one-digit number such as 7; or 0 (which is highly unlikely but possible).

4. Explain that after a student finds a number, he is to record it on his "Three-Digit Number Comparison Sheet" under "My Numbers." His partner will record the number on her sheet under "My Partner's Number." (Note: For groups of three, students should take turns. For example, Student A compares numbers with Student B, Student C compares numbers with Student A, Student C compares numbers with Student B, and the procedure repeats.)

5. Explain that after both students have thrown their die and recorded the numbers, they are to compare the numbers and use the symbols >, =, or < to create a math sentence such as 879 > 23. They should work individually when writing their comparisons and then compare their answers. They should discuss any answers for which they do not agree and make any necessary corrections. Explain to students that even though the order of the numbers and the "greater than" and "less than" symbols are opposite to what their partner has written on his or her sheet, the same information is being conveyed; 879 > 23 conveys the same information as 23 < 879.

6. Explain that students should compare ten pairs of numbers. (If you wish to extend the activity, hand out an additional comparison sheet.)

CLOSURE

Check your students' work. Have pairs of students write some examples of their comparisons on the board.

Name _____

THREE-DIGIT NUMBER COMPARISON SHEET

Directions: Roll your die three times to make a number of up to three digits. Compare your number to your partner's number. Use the symbols >, =, or <.

My Numbers	>,=,<	My Partner's Numbers

1. _____

2. _____

3. _____

4. _____

5. _____

6. _____

7. _____

8. _____

9. _____

10. _____

Number and Operations in Base Ten: 2.NBT.5

"Use place value understanding and properties of operations to add and subtract."

> 5. "Fluently add and subtract within 100 using strategies based on place value, properties of operations, and/or the relationship between addition and subtraction."

BACKGROUND

Even in this day of superfast calculators, students need to be able to add and subtract (along with performing other basic operations in math). Practice leads to proficiency.

ACTIVITY: ADDITION AND SUBTRACTION BINGO WITHIN 100

Students will receive a bingo board on which they will randomly write the answers to addition and subtraction problems. The answers are provided on the bottom of the board. The teacher will present the problems, and students will solve the problems and then find the answers on their boards, covering each answer with a counter. The first student to cover five answers in a row, column, or along a diagonal wins.

MATERIALS

25 counters; reproducible, "Addition and Subtraction Bingo within 100," for each student; reproducible, "Bingo Problems—Adding and Subtracting within 100," for the teacher.

PROCEDURE

1. Explain that students will play a game called bingo. This game is a little different from the standard game, because you will present addition and subtraction problems that students will solve. They will find the answers to their problems on their bingo boards.

2. Hand out the materials. Explain that the bingo board contains 25 squares. Note that the center square is labeled "Free Space." Instruct your students to place a counter on this square. Next explain that 24 numbers are on the bottom of their bingo board. Students are to randomly write each number in one of the remaining spaces on their board. If necessary, tell your students that randomly means no special order. As students write a number, they should cross it out on the bottom of the sheet so that they do not inadvertently use the number again.

3. Explain the rules of the game. You will present a problem by saying it, for example, 24 + 67. (Depending on your students, you may find it helpful to write the problem on the board as well.) Students are to copy the problem on a sheet of paper and solve it. As soon as they solve a problem, they should look for the answer on their bingo board. All problems will have an answer on the board. When they find the answer, they are to cover it with a counter. The first student to cover five squares in a row, column, or along a diagonal should raise her hand and say "Bingo!" (Note: To keep the game moving, you might want to place a time limit, perhaps 30, 45, or 60 seconds, for students to complete a problem.)

4. Instruct your students not to remove their counters from their boards when someone says they have bingo until you check that the winner's answers are correct.

5. Begin the game. Use the problems from "Bingo Problems—Adding and Subtracting within 100." You may find it helpful to copy the page and read from that rather than read the problems from the page in the book. If after all the problems have been used and no one has gotten bingo, you might declare the student who has the most counters in a row, column, or diagonal the winner. You may play additional games on the same board by using the same problems, but changing their order, or creating new problems that match the answers on the board.

CLOSURE

Have your students check their boards and choose a row, column, or diagonal that is close to getting bingo. (Even the student who got bingo can do this.) Instruct your students to create addition or subtraction problems of their own that will result in the answer, or answers, that give them bingo.

Bingo Board

		FREE SPACE		

Number Bank

17	35	45	42	63	19	29	87
82	41	98	83	13	34	100	33
93	57	22	95	8	52	88	53

1) 26 +16 Answer: 42	2) 45 −23 Answer: 22	3) 87 −54 Answer: 33	4) 61 +27 Answer: 88	5) 53 −45 Answer: 8	6) 18 +65 Answer: 83
7) 25 +57 Answer: 82	8) 32 +25 Answer: 57	9) 85 −68 Answer: 17	10) 75 −34 Answer: 41	11) 15 +72 Answer: 87	12) 93 −40 Answer: 53
13) 57 −23 Answer: 34	14) 18 +17 Answer: 35	15) 65 +30 Answer: 95	16) 48 +45 Answer: 93	17) 73 −54 Answer: 19	18) 86 −34 Answer: 52
19) 19 +26 Answer: 45	20) 77 −64 Answer: 13	21) 91 −28 Answer: 63	22) 59 +39 Answer: 98	23) 62 −33 Answer: 29	24) 30 +70 Answer:100

Number and Operations in Base Ten: 2.NBT.6

"Use place value understanding and properties of operations to add and subtract."

> 6. "Add up to four two-digit numbers using strategies based on place value and properties of operations."

BACKGROUND

Adding multiple numbers requires the use of the commutative and associative properties. Understanding place value is important, because when adding, students must start with the digits in the ones place. They can add or group these digits in any order and then follow the same procedure to add the digits in the tens place.

ACTIVITY: MAKING ADDITION PROBLEMS

Working in pairs or groups of three, students will be given a set of numbers that they will use to create two addition problems, each with four two-digit numbers. They will create a problem that has the largest sum and a problem that has the smallest sum.

MATERIALS

Scissors; reproducible, "Numbers for Making Addition Problems," for each pair or group of students.

PROCEDURE

1. Hand out the materials. Explain that the reproducible contains the numbers 1 to 9. Students are to cut out the numbers and arrange them into four two-digit numbers that when added will result in the largest sum. Then they are to rearrange the numbers into four two-digit numbers that when added will result in the smallest sum. Cutting the numbers out allows students to mix the numbers in various ways as they work to find the required sums. For each sum, one number will not be used.

2. Offer your students this hint: Place value is the key to finding the two-digit numbers that will result in the biggest sum and smallest sum.

3. Explain that after they find the four two-digit numbers that result in the largest sum, they should record the problem on a sheet of paper. After they find the four two-digit numbers that result in the smallest sum, they should record this problem on their paper.

CLOSURE

Ask your students what four two-digit numbers they found that result in the largest sum, which is 314. There are various combinations. One combination is $95 + 84 + 73 + 62 = 314$. Other combinations that will result in 314 include any four numbers in which 9, 8, 7, and 6 are in the tens place and 5, 4, 3, and 2 are in the ones place.

Ask your students what four two-digit numbers when added result in the smallest sum, which is 126. Again, various combinations are possible. One combination is $15 + 26 + 37 + 48 = 126$. Other combinations include any four numbers in which 1, 2, 3, and 4 are in the tens place and 5, 6, 7, and 8 are in the ones place.

Ask your students how understanding place value can help to solve these kinds of problems.

1	2	3
4	5	6
7	8	9

Number and Operations in Base Ten: 2.NBT.7

"Use place value understanding and properties of operations to add and subtract."

7. "Add and subtract within 1,000, using concrete models or drawings and strategies based on place value, properties of operations, and/or the relationship between addition and subtraction; relate the strategy to a written method. Understand that in adding or subtracting three-digit numbers, one adds or subtracts hundreds and hundreds, tens and tens, ones and ones; and sometimes it is necessary to compose or decompose tens or hundreds."

BACKGROUND

Until students master addition and subtraction, they can benefit from using models, drawings, and various strategies. Being able to explain a strategy in writing is a sign that students have fully mastered the process.

 ACTIVITY: CREATING DRAWINGS THAT REPRESENT ADDITION AND SUBTRACTION

Working in pairs or groups of three, students will be given a three-digit addition problem and a three-digit subtraction problem. They will create drawings to model the problems, solve the problems, and write an explanation of the strategies they used. (Note: You may prefer to present this activity in two sessions.)

MATERIALS

Scissors; crayons; glue sticks; 1 sheet of large drawing paper; reproducible, "Place Value Patterns," for each pair or group of students; card stock for the teacher.

PREPARATION

Make copies of the reproducible on card stock.

PROCEDURE

1. Hand out the materials. Explain that the reproducible contains three figures that can be used to represent the place value of each digit in a number. (You may liken the figures to base ten blocks.) The figures are labeled—the big square contains 100 square units and represents 100, the rectangle contains 10 square units and represents 10, and the small square represents 1.

2. Instruct your students to carefully cut out each figure and place the figures side by side in order, 100, 10, and 1. Ask what number the figures, if added together, represent. Students should realize the answer is 111.

3. Explain that students can represent bigger numbers by tracing multiple copies of the figures. For example, two of the 100 figures would represent 200, five of the 10 figures would represent 50, and nine of the 1 figures would represent 9.

4. Explain that you will assign each pair or group of students an addition and subtraction problem. They are to solve the problems and then create drawings that represent the problems. To create their drawings, they should trace the figures that they cut out. For example, to represent the number 325, they would trace three copies of the 100 figure, two copies of the 10 figure, and five copies of the 1 figure on their paper. (Note: Students need not attempt to draw 100 units on the large square or 10 units on the rectangle. Rather they may simply write 100 and 10 in each figure, respectively.)

5. Assign different pairs of problems to each pair or group of students. You may assign problems of your own or assign the following. Note that the answers to the problems are in parentheses.

1. 286 + 437 (723)   983 − 642 (341)
2. 495 + 278 (773)   816 − 421 (395)
3. 227 + 653 (880)   706 − 231 (475)
4. 463 + 438 (901)   774 − 208 (566)
5. 246 + 359 (605)   937 − 698 (239)
6. 196 + 683 (879)   747 − 323 (424)
7. 509 + 449 (958)   565 − 418 (147)
8. 238 + 154 (392)   860 − 245 (615)
9. 488 + 185 (673)   692 − 345 (347)
10. 412 + 381 (793)   489 − 327 (162)
11. 562 + 374 (936)   864 − 652 (212)
12. 386 + 408 (794)   427 − 109 (318)
13. 267 + 565 (832)   598 − 327 (271)
14. 378 + 429 (807)   925 − 568 (357)
15. 726 + 159 (885)   905 − 686 (219)

6. Instruct your students to start with their addition problem. They should represent the problem by using their patterns to draw the blocks for each number. Then they should solve the problem and write the solution next to their drawing. They are to also write an explanation of the strategies or methods they used to solve the problem. They should write their explanations on lined paper, cut out the explanation, and glue it next to the problem and drawing. Encourage students to color their drawings. They should follow this same procedure for their subtraction problem. Remind students to use a light color to fill

in the blocks representing the larger number of the subtraction problem and a darker color to show the subtrahend. (Note: For some pairs of problems, students may need an additional sheet of paper.)

CLOSURE

Check your students' work. Have students share their work with other pairs and groups of students. Discuss how the drawings are related to place value and represent the problems. Ask volunteers to share their problems and written explanations of the solutions with the class. Display your students' work.

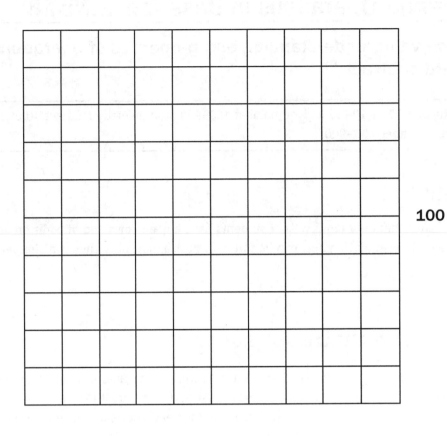

100

10

1

Number and Operations in Base Ten: 2.NBT.8

"Use place value understanding and properties of operations to add and subtract."

> 8. "Mentally add 10 or 100 to a given number 100–900, and mentally subtract 10 or 100 from a given number 100–900."

BACKGROUND

To add and subtract mentally requires that students have a good command of addition and subtraction facts. Mental math games can be fun, but most importantly they can sharpen students' math skills.

 ACTIVITY: MENTAL MATH GO AROUND

Working in pairs or groups of three or four, students will play a game in which they pick cards and use a spinner to create problems that they must add or subtract mentally. The students in each group play against each other, receiving 1 point for each correct answer. The student with the most points at the end of the game is the winner.

MATERIALS

Scissors; 1 spinner (a blank spinner that has been divided into two sections and labeled with a + and −); reproducibles, "Mental Math Cards 100 to 900" and "Mental Math Cards 10 and 100," for each pair or group of students; reproducible, "Mental Math 100 to 900 Score Sheet," for each student.

PREPARATION

Divide blank spinners into two equal sections. Write an addition sign, +, on one section and a subtraction sign, −, on the other section. Copying reproducibles "Mental Math Cards 100 to 900" and "Mental Math Cards 10 and 100" on different colors of paper will make it easier to keep the sets separate.

PROCEDURE

1. Explain that students will play a game in which they will pick cards and mentally add 10 or 100 to a number from 100 to 900. They will use a spinner to determine whether they add or subtract.

2. Hand out the materials. Instruct your students to cut out both sets of number cards, keeping each set in a separate pile. They should shuffle each set and place them face down. Explain that all students have their own score sheet on which they are to record the problems of each group member. In this way, each student maintains a record of the group's work. Note that there is space for two problems on each line.

3. Instruct your students to write the name of each player in their group on their score sheets. The player who begins the game is player 1, the next player is player 2, and so on. In the case of a game with only two or three students, the spaces for additional players are left blank.

4. Explain the rules of the game. Player 1 starts. **She** picks a card from the mental math cards in the pile 100 to 900. She then spins the spinner to find whether her problem will be addition or subtraction (based upon spinning a + or −). Next she picks a card from the pile of mental math cards 10 and 100. If she picks a 10 and her spinner landed on +, she must mentally add 10 to the first number she picked. If she picks a 10 and her spinner landed on −, she must mentally subtract 10 from the first number she picked.

5. Explain that now the student must say her answer. At this point, all students in the group record her answer on their score sheets by writing 1 for player 1 and then write the problem, for example: $639 + 100 = 739$. The other members in her group now must decide if she is correct. If all students decide that she is correct, she receives 1 point for this problem. To record the point, students may write and circle a 1 after the problem. If, however, some members of the group disagree about the answer, group members are to work out the problem on a separate sheet of paper to find the correct answer. You may need to serve as referee when students are unable to agree on the answer. If the player's answer is wrong, she does not receive a point. After player 1 is finished, player 2 takes his turn and follows the same procedure. Player 2's player number, problem, answer, and scored point (if he answered the problem correctly) should be written in the next blank. The game ends when all cards have been used.

6. In the case of groups of three students, to make sure that all students have the same number of chances to score points, suggest that after all the cards have been used, the third player reshuffles the cards (keeping them in separate piles) and then takes another turn. For groups of 4, to provide more opportunities for students to score points, suggest that after they use all the cards, they reshuffle the cards and continue playing. Of course, you may suggest that all pairs and groups play additional games by reshuffling the cards. Pass out additional score sheets, if necessary.

CLOSURE

Check your students' answers and discuss any problems that they had difficulty with. Have them tally their scores so that you may announce the winners of each group.

Reinforce mental math skills by presenting some more problems, such as $259 + 100$, and asking volunteers to provide the answer.

220	555	780	363
860	648	491	107
269	314	725	540
901	874	437	196
511	284	386	700

10	100	100	10
10	100	10	100
100	10	100	10
100	100	10	10
100	10	10	100

Name _____

MENTAL MATH 100 TO 900 SCORE SHEET

Directions: Write the name of the player after each player's number. Then record the problems and answers for each player.

Player 1: _____   Player 2: _____

Player 3: _____   Player 4: _____

_____   _____

_____   _____

_____   _____

_____   _____

_____   _____

_____   _____

_____   _____

Number and Operations in Base Ten: 2.NBT.9

"Use place value understanding and properties of operations to add and subtract."

> 9. "Explain why addition and subtraction strategies work, using place value and the properties of operations."

BACKGROUND

Students may be able to add and subtract without understanding why addition and subtraction operations work. These students come to recognize the sums and differences of specific numbers; for example, $6 + 5 = 11$. But only when students understand the operations of addition and subtraction do they gain mastery of these skills.

 ## ACTIVITY: EXPLAINING ADDITION AND SUBTRACTION OPERATIONS

Working in groups of three to five, students will be given an addition or subtraction problem. Each group will solve their problem and formulate an explanation of why addition or subtraction operations work, using their problem as an example. They will share their explanations with the class.

MATERIALS

Large index cards for each group of students.

PROCEDURE

1. Hand out the index cards. Explain that you will present each group with an addition or subtraction problem. Groups will receive different problems.

2. Explain that each group is to solve the problem they receive. They are to then discuss the problem and formulate an explanation of why the strategy they used to solve the problem works. For example, their explanation may include that when adding, you must first add ones to ones, then tens to tens, and then hundreds to hundreds. Students may also explain why in some cases it is necessary to compose and decompose tens and hundreds.

3. Next, explain that groups are to write their explanation on index cards, which they may use to refer to when sharing their explanation with the class. Offer the following suggestions for using index cards:

- Number their cards to keep them in order.

- List the main ideas of their explanations so that they may refer to them as they present their explanations.

- Write brief sentences; write neatly.

- Leave a blank line between sentences so that the cards are easier to read.

4. Present the following problems, or problems of your own, one problem to each group. Ideally, you should provide an equal number of addition and subtraction problems. The answers are provided in parentheses.

1. $264 + 128$ (392)
2. $156 + 275$ (431)
3. $227 + 182$ (409)
4. $293 + 150$ (443)
5. $384 - 263$ (121)
6. $425 - 114$ (311)
7. $368 - 249$ (119)
8. $325 - 167$ (158)

5. Confer with each group and discuss their explanation before they present it to the class. Tell each group to appoint a spokesperson, or spokespersons, to present their explanations.

6. Provide time for groups to practice their presentations.

CLOSURE

Have each group come to the front of the class one at a time, write their problem and its solution on the board, and share their explanation of why the strategy they used to solve the problem works. Suggest that they refer to their problem as an example as they present their explanation.

Measurement and Data: 2.MD.1

"Measure and estimate lengths in standard units."

1. "Measure the length of an object by selecting and using appropriate tools such as rulers, yardsticks, meter sticks, and measuring tapes."

BACKGROUND

When measuring lengths, students must learn to use the appropriate tools to obtain accurate results. Being able to select the appropriate tool is essential. Rulers are best for measuring relatively short lengths, while yardsticks and meter sticks are best used for measuring longer lengths. Measuring tapes are useful for measuring curves as well as straight lines.

 ACTIVITY: MEASURING OBJECTS WITH THE APPROPRIATE TOOLS

Working in groups of three or four, students will measure various objects in the classroom. They will select and use the appropriate tools from among rulers, yardsticks, meter sticks, and measuring tapes.

MATERIALS

1 ruler (with 12-inch and 30-centimeter scales); 1 yardstick; 1 meter stick; 1 cloth or metal measuring tape; reproducible, "Measurement Recording Sheet," for each group of students.

PROCEDURE

1. Hand out the materials. Explain that the reproducible contains eight objects students are to measure, as well as two objects of their choice in the classroom. Students will select the appropriate measuring tool to measure each object.

2. If necessary, discuss the measuring tools your students will use for this activity—the ruler (with both inch and centimeter scales), yardstick, meter stick, and measuring tape—and the practicality of using each. For example, a ruler (using inches or centimeters) should be used to measure the length of a crayon, while the height of a door should be measured with a yardstick or meter stick. Be sure your students are familiar with how to use each tool.

3. Explain that students are to select the best tool for measuring each object and then measure the object to the nearest whole unit. (Depending on your students, you might feel it is beneficial to explain and demonstrate what the term "to the nearest whole unit" means,

or you may prefer that they measure to the nearest half unit.) After measuring an object, they are to record their results on the recording sheet by writing the length of the object and the tool they used. (Your students might find it helpful if you write the name of each tool on the board.) They should be ready to explain their reasons for choosing the various tools.

CLOSURE

Discuss your students' results, noting that results may vary. For example, some objects may be measured by both a yardstick and a meter stick. Ask questions, such as the following:

- Which tool was the best for measuring each object? Why was it the best?

- Why might students have gotten different measurements for the same object?

- How might using different tools result in different measurements for the same object?

- Why would some tools—for example, a 1-foot ruler (using the inch scale) and yardstick—result in the same measurements?

- How do you decide what is the best tool for measuring an object?

Names _____

MEASUREMENT RECORDING SHEET

Directions: Measure and record the length of each object below. Choose the best tool for measuring each one.

Object	Length	Measuring Tool
1) An eraser		
2) A student's arm		
3) Distance around a shoe		
4) A pencil		
5) A book		
6) A student (head to toe)		
7) A desk		
8) A windowsill		

Measure two objects of your choice in the classroom.

9)		
10)		

Measurement and Data: 2.MD.2

"Measure and estimate lengths in standard units."

2. "Measure the length of an object twice, using length units of different lengths for the two measurements; describe how the two measurements relate to the size of the unit chosen."

BACKGROUND

Although the length of an object remains constant, measuring it with different length units will result in different measurements. Young students must learn to interpret measures accurately, particularly from different units.

 ACTIVITY: MEASUREMENTS AND LENGTH UNITS

Working in pairs or groups of three, students will measure the length of a textbook using two different length units.

MATERIALS

Scissors; crayons; a textbook; reproducible, "Two Different Length Units," for each pair or group of students.

PROCEDURE

1. Hand out the materials. Explain that length units can be used to measure the length of an object. The reproducible contains two different length units, ten of each unit. (Note: The longer unit is $2\frac{1}{2}$ inches in length and the shorter unit is $1\frac{1}{4}$ inches in length.)

2. Explain that students are to cut out the length units. They may color them, but the larger units should all be the same color, perhaps green, and the smaller units should all be the same color, maybe red.

3. Instruct your students to take a book, such as their math text. Every pair or group of students should use a copy of the same book.

4. Instruct your students to place the book on their desk in order to measure its length. If necessary, point out that the book's length can be measured by measuring one of its longer sides. Students are to measure the length to the nearest unit, using their longer length units. On a sheet of paper, they should write how many units the length of the book is. They are to measure the book's length to the nearest unit again, this time using the shorter length units, and then write down the number of units they used. Depending on

your students, you might feel it is beneficial to explain and demonstrate what the term "to the nearest unit" means.

CLOSURE

Discuss your students' results. Ask questions such as the following:

- How many of the longer length units did you use to measure the length of the book? Did anyone find a different number? How might this have happened?

- How many of the smaller length units did you use to measure the length of the book? Did anyone find a different number? What might be the reason for this?

- How are the two length units related? (Students should answer that the longer one is two times the length of the shorter one, or the shorter one is $\frac{1}{2}$ the length of the longer one.)

To extend the activity, have students measure the length of another object.

Measurement and Data: 2.MD.3

"Measure and estimate lengths in standard units."

3. "Estimate lengths using units of inches, feet, centimeters, and meters."

BACKGROUND

Being able to estimate the length of an object is a useful skill, especially in instances when measuring tools are unavailable or an exact measurement is not necessary. Estimating the lengths of objects improves with practice.

 ACTIVITY: ESTIMATING LENGTHS

Working in pairs or groups of three, students will estimate the length of objects in inches, feet, centimeters, and meters. They will record their results and then measure the objects. They will compare their estimates with actual measurements.

MATERIALS

A ruler (with 12-inch and 30-centimeter scales); a yardstick; a meter stick; reproducible, "Estimates and Measurements Worksheet," for each pair or group of students; 10 large index cards; 1 dark marker; masking tape for the teacher.

PREPARATION

Select 10 objects around the classroom whose length students will estimate and then measure. Objects may include the lengths of bulletin boards, desks, window sills, books, pencils, crayons, erasers, floor tiles, staplers, glue sticks, sheets of large paper, sheets of small paper, and so on. (Be sure to measure the length of each object yourself.) Choose five objects that are best measured in inches or centimeters and five objects that are best measured in feet or meters. Write the names of the objects on the worksheet, with numbers 1 to 5 for objects measured in inches and centimeters and numbers 6 to 10 for objects measured in feet and inches.

Mark ten locations where students will find the objects. Write the number and name of the object (matching its number and name on the reproducible) on an index card and tape the card near the object.

1. Hand out the materials. Review the different measuring tools and their units of measure. If necessary, review the use of the tools.

2. Explain that for this activity students are to first estimate the lengths of objects and then measure the objects and compare the measurements to their estimates. Point out the ten objects (and their locations) that students are to measure. Note that the objects are numbered.

3. To help your students make their estimates, point out how long an inch is, how long a centimeter is, how long a foot is, and how long a meter is. Provide some examples of objects that could be measured in inches, centimeters, feet, yards, and meters (though not the objects you placed on the worksheet). Ask your students to estimate the lengths of these objects and then tell them the actual measurements. These will serve as benchmarks and help students to estimate the lengths of other objects.

4. Explain that the objects they are to estimate and measure are listed on their worksheet. Each pair or group of students is to estimate the length of each object, in inches and centimeters for problems 1 to 5 and feet and meters for problems 6 to 10. They should discuss and agree on their estimate before recording it on their paper. After they record an estimate, they are to measure the object, using the appropriate tools, and record its actual length.

5. To ensure smooth movement throughout the classroom, start the activity by having pairs and groups of students estimate and measure different objects. Instruct students to go to objects in order from the number they start with on their worksheets. For example, students who start with object 1 should next go to object 2, then 3, and so on. The students who start with object 2 should next go to object 3, then 4, and eventually finish with object 1. The students who start with object 10 should next go to object 1, then 2, and eventually finish with object 9. Remind students to make sure that they write their estimates and measurements in the correct places on their worksheets.

CLOSURE

Discuss your students' estimates and actual measurements, as well as the tools they used to measure the different objects. Ask: Whose estimate (for a particular object) was very close to its actual measurement? Whose estimate was very different? By how much? Find out if different pairs and groups of students had different measurements for the same objects. Why might this be?

ESTIMATES AND MEASUREMENTS WORKSHEET

Directions: Estimate the length of each object below. Then measure the object to find its length.

Object	Estimated Length	Actual Length
1)	Inches: Centimeters:	Inches: Centimeters:
2)	Inches: Centimeters:	Inches: Centimeters:
3)	Inches: Centimeters:	Inches: Centimeters:
4)	Inches: Centimeters:	Inches: Centimeters:
5)	Inches: Centimeters:	Inches: Centimeters:
6)	Feet: Meters:	Feet: Meters:
7)	Feet: Meters:	Feet: Meters:
8)	Feet: Meters:	Feet: Meters:
9)	Feet: Meters:	Feet: Meters:
10)	Feet: Meters:	Feet: Meters:

Measurement and Data: 2.MD.4

"Measure and estimate lengths in standard units."

> 4. "Measure to determine how much longer one object is than another, expressing the length difference in terms of a standard length unit."

BACKGROUND

Inches, feet, yards, centimeters, and meters are examples of standard length units. When measured with the same standard length unit, the lengths of objects can be easily compared. For example, a board that is 5 feet long is 4 feet longer than a board that is 1 foot long. Length units must be consistent to serve as a means of comparison. Inches cannot be compared to feet and centimeters cannot be compared to meters (unless they are converted). Once students are able to measure the length of objects using the same length units, they can subtract to find the difference in length.

ACTIVITY: EXPRESSING DIFFERENCES IN LENGTHS

Working in pairs or groups of three, students will measure four ribbons of different lengths. They will express the differences in lengths in terms of a 1-inch length unit.

MATERIALS

Ruler with 1-inch scale; 4 ribbons of different colors and lengths; reproducible, "Ribbon Lengths and Measurement," for each pair or group of students.

PREPARATION

For each pair or group of students, cut four lengths of different-colored ribbons—blue, green, red, and white. Cut the blue ribbon into 12-inch strips; cut the green ribbon into 8-inch strips; cut the red ribbon into 6-inch strips; and cut the white ribbon into 4-inch strips. Cut enough strips so that each pair or group of students has one ribbon of each color.

PROCEDURE

1. Hand out the materials. Explain that students have four ribbons, cut into four different lengths. They are to measure the ribbons with their rulers, with 1 inch being their standard length unit, and then answer the questions on the worksheet based on their measurements.

2. To make sure that your students understand what to do, instruct them to measure the blue ribbon. Ask: How long is the ribbon? They should find that it is 12 inches. Students are to measure the other ribbons in the same way as they answer the questions on their worksheets.

CLOSURE

Discuss your students' answers. Ask them how using a standard length unit makes it easy to compare the lengths of different objects.

ANSWERS

(1) 12 inches **(2)** 6 inches **(3)** 6 inches **(4)** 8 inches **(5)** 4 inches **(6)** 2 inches **(7)** 4 inches **(8)** 8 inches **(9)** 4 inches **(10)** 2 inches

Names _____

RIBBON LENGTHS AND MEASUREMENT

Directions: Answer the questions.

1. How long is the blue ribbon? _____

2. How long is the red ribbon? _____

3. How much longer is the blue ribbon than the red ribbon? _____

4. How long is the green ribbon? _____

5. How much longer is the blue ribbon than the green ribbon? _____

6. How much longer is the green ribbon than the red ribbon? _____

7. How long is the white ribbon? _____

8. How much longer is the blue ribbon than the white ribbon? _____

9. How much longer is the green ribbon than the white ribbon? _____

10. How much longer is the red ribbon than the white ribbon? _____

Measurement and Data: 2.MD.5

"Relate addition and subtraction to length."

> 5. "Use addition and subtraction within 100 to solve word problems involving lengths that are given in the same units, e.g., by using drawings (such as drawings of rulers) and equations with a symbol for the unknown number to represent the problem."

BACKGROUND

Solving word problems is challenging for many students because of the various skills required. Students must be able to read the problem, identify what it is asking, decide on the mathematical operation to solve the problem, and perform the necessary computation to find the answer. Drawings and equations can often be helpful for clarifying the data in a word problem.

ACTIVITY: SOLVING MEASUREMENT WORD PROBLEMS

Students will solve addition and subtraction measurement word problems within 100. They will draw pictures and write equations with a symbol for the unknown number to represent the problem.

MATERIALS

Crayons; unlined paper; reproducible, "Measurement Word Problems within 100," for each student.

PROCEDURE

1. Hand out the materials. Explain that students are to solve the six addition and subtraction word problems on the worksheet. They are also to draw a picture and write an equation to represent each problem, using a symbol in place of the unknown number.

2. Explain that to solve word problems, students must first read the problem carefully; reread the problem, if necessary; determine what the problem is asking them to find; decide on the mathematical operation to use—in this case, addition or subtraction—and then do the necessary computation. To help them clarify information in the problem, students may write an equation or draw a picture. They should also double-check their work and make sure that their answers make sense.

3. Start the first problem together as a class. Ask a volunteer to read the problem. Then ask the following questions:

- What is the problem asking you to find? (How much higher the oak tree is than the maple tree.)

- How might you draw a picture that represents the problem? (Students might suggest drawing two trees, a taller one and labeling it 48 feet and a shorter one and labeling it 36 feet.) Your students might find it helpful if you sketched a picture on the board showing how they could label the trees by drawing a line next to each one and writing its height.

- What operation is needed to solve the problem? (Subtraction, 48 feet minus 36 feet)

- What equation can you write with a symbol for the unknown number to represent this problem? ($48 - 36 = ?$)

4. Instruct your students to complete this problem and then finish the other problems on the worksheet. They should do their work on unlined paper, and include a drawing and an equation with each problem.

CLOSURE

Check your students' answers. Ask for examples of pictures they drew and equations they wrote to represent the problems. Discuss any problems your students found difficult to solve.

ANSWERS

Drawings will vary; equations and solutions follow. (**1**) $48 - 36 = ?$; 12 feet (**2**) $32 + 17 = ?$; 49 inches (**3**) $66 + 24 = ?$; 90 inches (**4**) $76 - 58 = ?$; 18 centimeters (**5**) $61 - 45 = ?$; 16 meters (**6**) $28 + 22 = ?$; 50 centimeters

Name _____

MEASUREMENT WORD PROBLEMS WITHIN 100

Directions: Solve the problems.

1. An oak tree is 48 feet high. A maple tree nearby is 36 feet high. How much higher is the oak tree than the maple tree?

2. A young kangaroo was 32 inches tall. It grew 17 inches. How tall is the kangaroo now?

3. A flower garden was 66 inches long. Mary helped her father add 24 inches to its length. How long is the flower garden now?

4. Sara had 76 centimeters of ribbon. She used 58 centimeters to wrap a present. How much ribbon did she have left?

5. Tom ran 61 meters. William ran 45 meters. How many more meters did Tom run than William?

6. Emma placed 28 centimeter cubes end to end to make a line of cubes. She added 22 more centimeter cubes to the line. How long is the line of centimeter cubes now?

Measurement and Data: 2.MD.6

"Relate addition and subtraction to length."

> 6. "Represent whole numbers as lengths from 0 on a number line diagram with equally spaced points corresponding to the numbers 0, 1, 2, ..., and represent whole-number sums and differences within 100 on a number line diagram."

BACKGROUND

Number line diagrams are useful for representing relationships between numbers. For example, students can construct number line diagrams to represent addition and subtraction of whole numbers by making "jumps" to the right to show addition and "jumps" to the left to show subtraction.

ACTIVITY: CONSTRUCTING NUMBER LINE DIAGRAMS TO SHOW ADDITION AND SUBTRACTION

Students will construct number line diagrams to represent solutions to addition and subtraction problems.

MATERIALS

Reproducible, "Number Line Diagrams—Addition and Subtraction," for each student; scissors or paper cutter and reproducible, "Tick Mark Rulers," for the teacher. Optional: Card stock on which to copy "Tick Mark Rulers."

PREPARATION

Make enough copies of the reproducible "Tick Mark Rulers" so that each student will have his or her own ruler. The reproducible contains five rulers. Cut out each ruler from the reproducible.

PROCEDURE

1. Explain that a number line diagram is a line with equally spaced marks called ticks that are named by numbers. Provide some examples on the board, such as the following:

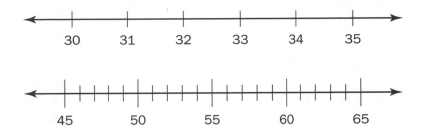

2. Explain that a number line diagram does not always begin at 0. You might also want to explain that the line (and numbers) go on in both directions infinitely.

3. Hand out the materials. Explain that the worksheet contains an example problem, two addition problems, and two subtraction problems that students are to solve and then represent on number line diagrams. A number line is located below each problem. For problem 1, the number line diagram is provided. For problem 2, the number line diagram is partially provided. For problems 3 and 4, students must construct the number line diagrams, using their tick mark ruler as a guide to help them divide the number lines into a sufficient number of equally spaced intervals.

4. Direct your students' attention to the example and work through the problem as a class to help them get started.

    • Instruct your students to solve the problem. They should find the answer to be 47.

    • Explain that students are to now represent the sum on the number line diagram. It is started for them and begins with the number 30 and includes tick marks. But only the number 30 is labeled. Tell your students to count the tick marks, labeling them in multiples of 5, for example, 30, 35, 40, and so on. Note that the tick marks that end in a multiple of 5 are slightly longer than the others, which makes counting and labeling easier. What number do they end with? Students should find that it is 50. Instruct them to place their tick mark ruler on the number line. They should realize that the tick marks on the number line coincide with the tick marks on their ruler. (Note: The tick mark ruler is longer than the ruler for the example.) They will use the ruler later to make tick marks on problems 3 and 4.

    • Ask your students how they could represent adding 15 to 32 on their number line. Students should start at 32, draw a curved line that "jumps" 15 spaces to the right and lands on 47. Have them draw the line on their number line diagrams.

    • Ask your students how they could represent subtraction on a number line diagram. They should realize that a number line diagram representing subtraction would start with the larger number and "jump" to the left as many spaces as the number being subtracted.

5. Explain that students are to solve the rest of the problems on the worksheet and complete the number line diagram representing the solution for each problem. Remind them to use their tick mark rulers to divide the number line diagrams for problems 3 and 4.

CLOSURE

Discuss your students' results. Sketch a number line diagram on the board with tick marks, but without numbers. Have students come up and complete the number line diagram, showing the solution to each problem on the worksheet.

ANSWERS

(**1**) 52—The number line diagram begins at 25 and ends at 55. Starting at 27, a curved line is drawn 25 tick marks to the right and stops at 52. (**2**) 28—The number line diagram begins at 25 and ends at 60. Starting at 59, a curved line is drawn 31 tick marks to the left and stops at 28. (**3**) 97—The number line diagram begins at 65 and ends at 100. Starting at 68, a curved line is drawn 29 tick marks to the right and stops at 97. (**4**) 54—The number line diagram begins at 50 and ends at 85. Starting at 82, a curved line is drawn to the left 28 tick marks and stops at 54.

Name _____

NUMBER LINE DIAGRAMS—ADDITION AND SUBTRACTION

Directions: Solve the problems. Complete a number line diagram to represent each problem.

Example: 32
                +15

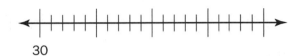

30

1. 27
       +25

25   30   35   40   45   50   55

2. 59
       −31

25   60

3. 68
       +29

4. 82
       −28

TICK MARK RULERS

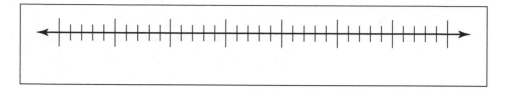

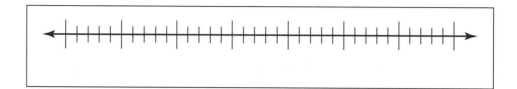

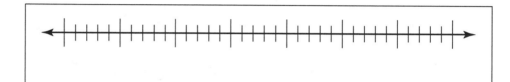

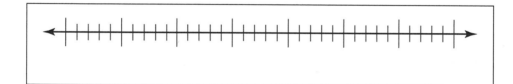

Measurement and Data: 2.MD.7

"Work with time and money."

7. "Tell and write time from analog and digital clocks to the nearest five minutes, using a.m. and p.m."

BACKGROUND

As they advance through second grade, students should master telling time accurately on both analog and digital clocks. They should also understand that a.m. (ante meridiem) denotes morning times, before noon, and p.m. (post meridiem) denotes times after noon, until the next morning begins. (Note: Students need not know the formal terms.)

ACTIVITY 1: TIME ON THE INTERNET

Using a Web site, the teacher leads an activity in which students answer questions using virtual digital and analog clocks.

MATERIALS

Computer with Internet access; digital projector for the teacher.

PROCEDURE

1. Go to http://nlvm.usu.edu/. Click on "Pre-K–2," "Measurement," and then click on "Time-Match Clocks." You will see an analog clock and digital clock on the screen.

2. Explain to your students that you will present times on either the analog or the digital clock. Students are to match the time shown on this clock with the other clock. Students should raise their hands if they know the correct answer and you will call on them.

3. Demonstrate the activity. At the top of the screen, students will be told which clock has the time they are to match with the other clock. If the time they are to match appears on the analog clock, they are to find the time on the digital clock. If the time they are to match appears on the digital clock, they are to find the time on the analog clock.

4. For problems that require the time to be changed on the analog clock, simply click on and drag the clock's hands. To change the time on the digital clock, click on the up and down arrows beneath the clock.

5. To check students' answers, click on "Check Answer." If the time a student gives is incorrect, have another student try to match the correct time. Click on "New Problem" for another problem. Present several problems and have students say the correct time on the clock.

Explain to your students that analog clocks do not show a.m. or p.m. Explain that a.m. refers to times in the morning from after midnight (12:01 a.m.) until just before noon (11:59 a.m.), and that p.m. refers to times after noon (12:01 p.m.) until just before midnight (11:59 p.m.). If the time is exactly 12:00, the correct form is "noon" or "midnight."

 ## ACTIVITY 2: MATCHING TIME CARDS

Working in pairs or groups of three, students will cut out cards containing clocks and times. They will arrange the cards that show the same times and glue them in rows on a sheet of paper.

MATERIALS

Scissors; glue sticks; 1 sheet of 18-inch by 24-inch construction paper; reproducibles, "Analog Clocks" and "Times and Digital Clocks," for each pair or group of students.

PROCEDURE

1. Hand out the materials. Explain that the reproducibles contain cards with pictures of times on analog clocks, digital clocks, and times in words. The cards containing times in words are numbered 1 to 9. The cards containing the clocks are not numbered.

2. Explain that students are to cut out the cards and arrange them in rows so that the times are the same in each row. Each time is to be represented in words, on an analog clock, and on a digital clock.

3. Explain that students are to glue all three cards that represent the same time in a row on their paper. They should start the rows with the numbered cards that have times in words. The first row should start with card 1, the second row should start with card 2, the third row should start with card 3, and so on. Caution them to arrange all of the cards on their paper before gluing to make sure that they have enough space for the cards. If necessary, demonstrate how they can do this.

4. Explain that the digital clocks include a.m. and p.m. and that the cards containing words include a.m., p.m., "morning," "afternoon," or "evening." Explain that most analog clocks do not show a.m. or p.m.

CLOSURE

Check your students' work. Cards with clocks should match cards with time words. Have students share their work with other pairs or groups. Display students' work.

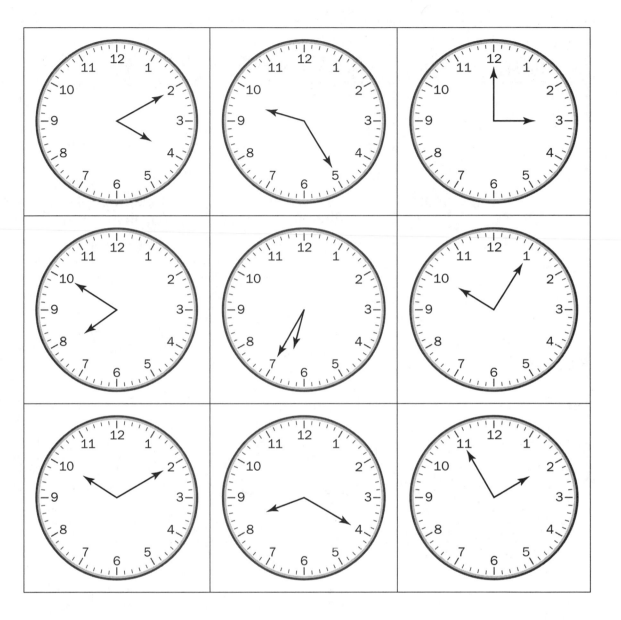

1. Three o'clock in the afternoon	2. Five minutes after ten a.m.	3. Twenty minutes after eight in the morning
4. Six thirty-five in the evening	5. Four ten in the afternoon	6. Nine twenty-five in the morning
7. One fifty-five p.m.	8. Ten ten in the morning	9. Seven fifty in the morning
9:25 AM	10:05 AM	4:10 PM
8:20 AM	1:55 PM	6:35 PM
3:00 PM	10:10 AM	7:50 AM

Measurement and Data: 2.MD.8

"Work with time and money."

> 8. "Solve word problems involving dollar bills, quarters, dimes, nickels, and pennies, using $ and ¢ symbols appropriately."

BACKGROUND

Understanding the value and use of money is an essential life skill. Solving word problems involving dollars and coins and expressing amounts correctly provides students with practice that will help them master concepts and operations with money.

ACTIVITY 1: A BOOK ABOUT MATH AND MONEY

The teacher reads the book *Pigs Will Be Pigs* to the class and discusses the money the characters find in the story.

MATERIALS

A copy of *Pigs Will Be Pigs* by Amy Axelrod (Aladdin, 1997).

PROCEDURE

1. Have your students sit around you so that you will be able to share the illustrations in the book with them as you read. Explain that the Pig family wants to go out to dinner because they are very hungry, but they have no food in the house. There is another problem, though—they have no money.

2. Read the story that tells how the Pig family searches through their house for money. As you read, pause and show the illustrations to your students, pointing out the bills and coins the family finds. Ask your students to try to keep track of all the money the Pig family finds. You might suggest that students write down the amounts on a sheet of paper.

3. When the Pigs get to the restaurant, share the menu with your students. Ask your students what they think the Pigs might order. What might your students order?

4. At the end of the story, review the money that the Pigs found in the house.

Have volunteers summarize the story. Ask questions, such as the following:

- How much money did the Pigs find in their house? Do you think this was a lot of money to find in a house? Do you think they could have found more? Where else might they have looked for money?

- What kinds of bills and coins did they find?

- Do you think the Pigs enjoyed their dinner? Why or why not?

- After they came home from the restaurant, what did the Pigs find?

 ## ACTIVITY 2: THE MONEY QUIZ GAME

Working in pairs or groups of three, students will play a game in which they must answer questions about money. Each pair or group competes as a team against other pairs and groups. At the end of the game, 1 point is awarded for each correct answer. The pair or group with the highest score wins.

MATERIALS

Reproducible, "Money Problems," for each pair or group of students. Optional: Classroom money (2 one-dollar bills, 8 quarters, 5 dimes, 5 nickels, 10 pennies) for each pair or group of students.

PROCEDURE

1. Explain that students will play a money game in which they will solve word problems involving dollar bills, quarters, dimes, nickels, and pennies. (Note: Students are not to use half dollars in this activity.) Each pair or group of students will play as a team against other pairs and groups. Each correct answer is worth 1 point.

2. Hand out the materials. (If you hand out the optional classroom money, explain that students may use the money to help them answer the questions.) Explain that the reproducible contains 12 problems that partners and group members are to answer. They are to confer about the answers and write their answer on a separate sheet of paper. Each pair or group of students must decide on one answer.

3. Suggest that students use scrap paper, if necessary, when solving the problems.

After everyone has finished, announce the answers. Students should correct their answer sheet and count 1 point for each correct answer. Announce the pairs or groups with the highest scores.

ANSWERS

(**1**) 6 quarters (**2**) $2.85 (**3**) 80¢ or $0.80 (**4**) 1 quarter, 1 nickel (**5**) 4 quarters, 1 dime (**6**) 3 quarters, 1 dime, 1 nickel (**7**) 10 pennies (**8**) 2 quarters, 1 dime, 1 nickel (**9**) 66¢ or $0.66 (**10**) $1.48 (**11**) 6 quarters, 2 nickels (**12**) 2 quarters, 1 dime

If there is a tie, present some tie-breaker problems (with a time limit), such as the following:

- 3 quarters, 1 dime, 1 nickel, and 3 pennies = _____. (93¢ or $0.93)
- 1 one-dollar bill, 1 quarter, 2 dimes, and 4 pennies = _____. ($1.49)
- 1 one-dollar bill, 2 quarters, 3 dimes, 1 nickel, and 1 penny = _____. ($1.86)
- 2 one-dollar bills, 1 quarter, 2 dimes, 1 nickel, and 4 pennies = _____. ($2.54)
- 2 quarters, 2 dimes, 2 nickels, and 7 pennies = _____. (87¢ or $0.87)

MONEY PROBLEMS

Directions: Solve each problem.

1) You have $1.52 in coins. What is the most quarters you can have?	**2)** You have 2 one-dollar bills, 3 quarters, and 2 nickels. How much money do you have?	**3)** You have 3 quarters, 2 dimes, and 1 nickel. You give 20¢ to a friend. How much money do you have left?
4) What 2 coins equal 30¢?	**5)** You have $1.10. What 5 coins do you have?	**6)** What 5 coins equal 90¢?
7) You have 10 coins that equal 1 dime. What coins do you have?	**8)** You have 65¢. What 4 coins do you have?	**9)** You have 1 quarter, 3 dimes, 2 nickels, and 1 penny. How much money do you have?
10) You have 1 one-dollar bill, 4 dimes, 1 nickel, and 3 pennies. How much money do you have?	**11)** You have $1.60. What 8 coins do you have?	**12)** You have 85¢. You give a quarter to a friend. What 3 coins do you have left?

Measurement and Data: 2.MD.9

"Represent and interpret data."

9. "Generate measurement data by measuring lengths of several objects to the nearest whole unit, or by making repeated measurements of the same object. Show the measurements by making a line plot, where the horizontal scale is marked off in whole-number lengths."

BACKGROUND

A line plot, sometimes called a dot plot, displays data along a number line. Each value of the data is marked with a symbol that shows its frequency.

For example, a line plot showing the lengths of eight randomly selected pencils to the nearest inch is shown below.

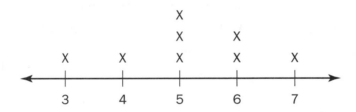

Note that an "X" is placed above the value each time the value appears.

 ACTIVITY: MEASUREMENT AND LINE PLOTS

Working in pairs or groups of three, students will cut out eight rectangles and measure their lengths to the nearest inch. They will construct a line plot to display the lengths of the rectangles.

MATERIALS

Scissors; rulers with a 1-inch scale; crayons; unlined paper; reproducible, "Rectangles," for each pair or group of students.

PROCEDURE

1. Explain that a line plot shows data along a number line. Each value of the data is marked with a symbol to show each time the data is counted. Provide examples of line plots, such as the one in the Background.

2. Hand out the materials. Explain that students will measure the lengths of eight rectangles and construct a line plot that shows the length of each rectangle. The rectangles are contained on the reproducible.

3. Instruct your students to cut out the rectangles. Note that each is labeled with a color. To make it easier to refer to the rectangles, have your students color the rectangles according to their labels. (Note: It may be easier to have students color the rectangles before cutting them out.)

4. Explain that students are to measure each rectangle to the nearest inch. Measure the green rectangle together as a class to ensure that students understand how they are to measure. Point out that the rectangle measures slightly more than 3 inches. Because the length is closer to 3 inches than 4 inches, students should record 3 inches for this rectangle's length. If the length was $3\frac{1}{2}$ inches to 4 inches, they would record 4 inches for the rectangle's length.

5. Tell your students to record the length of each rectangle on a sheet of paper. They will use this data to construct their line plots.

6. Explain how to construct a line plot. Students should do the following:

   - Use their ruler and draw a line about 6 inches long on their unlined paper. They should put an arrow on each end of the line to show that the line goes on infinitely.

   - Find the shortest and longest lengths of their data.

   - Place a small vertical line (a tick mark) near the left arrow on the line they drew. The small vertical line represents the shortest length of their data. Write this value under the tick mark.

   - Start at the small vertical line and use their ruler to mark off the line at intervals of 1 inch. Write the value under each tick mark.

   - Stop at the longest length of their data.

   - Place an "X" for every recorded length above its tick mark.

CLOSURE

Discuss the line plots. Ask your students questions such as the following:

- Which rectangle (or rectangles) had the longest length? (Orange and Violet, 7 inches)

- Which rectangle (or rectangles) had the shortest length? (Blue, 2 inches)

- What was the most common length (or lengths) they found? (Orange and Violet, 7 inches; Black and Yellow, 4 inches; Green and Red, 3 inches)

- What was the least common length (or lengths) they found? (Blue, 2 inches; Brown, 6 inches)

- Which length on their line plot had no value? (5 inches)

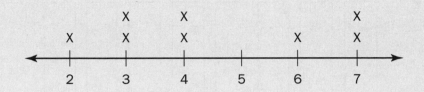

Black

Blue

Green

Red

Yellow

Brown

Orange

Violet

Measurement and Data: 2.MD.10

"Represent and interpret data."

10. "Draw a picture graph and a bar graph (with single-unit scale) to represent a data set with up to four categories. Solve simple put-together, take-apart, and compare problems using information presented in a bar graph."

BACKGROUND

Picture graphs and bar graphs are good visual models for showing data. A picture graph uses pictures to display data. A bar graph uses vertical or horizontal bars to display data. The same data set can often be shown on either a picture graph or a bar graph.

 ## ACTIVITY: CONSTRUCTING PICTURE GRAPHS AND BAR GRAPHS

This is a two-day activity. Working in pairs or groups of three, students will create a picture graph and a bar graph to represent a data set. You will conduct a poll of the class to generate the data (or you may present a data set of your own). Students will solve problems using information presented in the graphs.

MATERIALS

Unlined paper; rulers; crayons for each pair or group of students.

PREPARATION

Conduct a poll of your students on a familiar topic, limiting the categories to four. You might ask students to choose their favorite color (for example, red, blue, green, or yellow); their favorite pet (dog, cat, hamster, or bird); or their favorite sport (baseball, basketball, football, or soccer). You might select other topics or present data of your own to your students. Create put-together, take-apart, and compare problems based on the data, that students are to solve on day two of the activity.

Day One

1. If you choose to conduct a poll, write the results of the poll on the board using a frequency table, noting that each tally mark on the frequency table represents one response. Explain that the results are the data set students will use to construct a picture graph and a bar graph. Today students will construct a picture graph.

2. Explain that picture graphs use pictures to represent data. The value of each picture is shown on a legend on the graph. For example, a picture of a book might represent the number of students who have homework in a particular subject on a given night. Categories on a picture graph are labeled. Show your students examples of picture graphs in their math text or other books. You can also find numerous examples of picture graphs online by using the search term "picture graphs." Point out how picture graphs are constructed and how the pictures represent data.

3. Hand out the materials. Explain that students are to construct a picture graph using the data in the poll you conducted. Encourage them to provide the following in their graphs:

   - Choose a simple picture to represent the data in their picture graph; for example, a ball to represent a student's favorite sport or a crayon to represent a student's favorite color.

   - Create a legend for their picture graph, showing the quantity each picture represents. Suggest that each picture equals one or two items of data. For example, a picture of one crayon might represent one student's choice of a particular color. Two crayons would represent two students. Three crayons would represent three students, and so on. (Alternatively, one crayon could represent two students, two crayons could represent four students, and so on.)

   - Use their rulers to construct their graph.

   - Label each category.

   - Write a title for their picture graph.

   - Create neat and accurate work.

4. Collect the graphs.

Day Two

1. Explain that bar graphs show data using vertical or horizontal bars. The scale of a bar graph (usually along the side or bottom of the graph) represents numerical data. The bars are labeled. Show your students examples of bar graphs in their math text or other books. You may also find examples online by using the search term "bar graphs." Be sure to explain how the graph is constructed and how the scale represents the data.

2. Hand out the materials, including the picture graphs that students already completed. Explain that today students will make a bar graph, based on the data they used for their picture graphs. Encourage students to provide the following in their bar graphs:

- Create a scale for their bar graph. The scale should start at 0 and extend a little beyond the highest value of data. For large quantities of data, each unit of the scale might equal 2, 3, 4, or more. Suggest the scale that students should use for their graph.

- Use their rulers to construct their graph.

- Label each bar.

- Write a title for their bar graph.

- Create neat and accurate graphs.

3. After students have constructed their graphs, present the problems you created and instruct them to use their graphs to solve the problems.

CLOSURE

Check your students' graphs and discuss the answers to the problems. Ask your students how picture graphs and bar graphs are similar. How are they different? Which do they feel presents data more clearly? Which did they find easier to construct?

Display the graphs of your students.

Geometry: 2.G.1

"Reason with shapes and their attributes."

1. "Recognize and draw shapes having specified attributes, such as a given number of angles or a given number of equal faces. Identify triangles, quadrilaterals, pentagons, hexagons, and cubes."

BACKGROUND

Understanding that different shapes have different attributes enables students to recognize and identify shapes. Following are common shapes and their attributes:

- Triangle: A polygon that has three sides and three angles.
- Quadrilateral: A polygon that has four sides and four angles.
- Trapezoid: A quadrilateral that has exactly one pair of parallel sides.
- Parallelogram: A quadrilateral that has two pairs of parallel and congruent sides.
- Square: A quadrilateral that has four congruent sides and four right angles.
- Rectangle: A quadrilateral that has two pairs of parallel and congruent sides and four right angles.
- Pentagon: A polygon that has five sides and five angles.
- Hexagon: A polygon that has six sides and six angles.
- Cube: A three-dimensional shape that has six square faces.

ACTIVITY 1: IDENTIFYING AND CLASSIFYING SHAPES

Working in pairs or groups of three, students will cut out and match cards containing shapes and attributes. They will also name the shapes.

MATERIALS

Scissors; glue sticks; crayons; 1 sheet of 12-inch by 18-inch construction paper; reproducibles, "Shape Cards" and "Attribute Cards," for each pair or group of students.

PROCEDURE

1. Review common shapes and their attributes, as provided in the Background.

2. Distribute the materials. Explain that the cards on the reproducible "Shape Cards" contain various shapes. The shapes are numbered 1 to 9. The cards on the reproducible "Attribute

Cards" contain attributes that students will match with the shape cards. Students are to cut out the cards from both reproducibles.

3. Explain to your students that they are to first glue the attribute cards on their construction paper. They should arrange the attribute cards so that they have enough space below each one to glue the shape card (or cards) that matches it.

4. Explain that for each shape card students should write the name of the shape at the bottom of the card. You may suggest that students color the shapes. They should then glue each shape card under the attribute that applies to it. Some attribute cards apply to more than one shape.

CLOSURE

Check your students' work. Discuss how the number of sides, or, in the case of the cube, the number and kind of faces, of a shape are attributes that can be used to help identify and classify a shape.

ANSWERS

Names of the shapes: **(1)** Trapezoid **(2)** Triangle **(3)** Rectangle **(4)** Pentagon **(5)** Hexagon **(6)** Cube **(7)** Triangle **(8)** Square **(9)** Triangle

   For the attribute cards: Shapes that have 3 angles: triangles. Shapes that have 4 sides: trapezoid, rectangle, and square. A shape that has 5 sides: pentagon. A shape that has 6 sides: hexagon. A shape that has 6 square faces: cube.

ACTIVITY 2: DRAWING AND NAMING SHAPES

Students will be given the attributes of six shapes and will draw and name the shapes.

MATERIALS

Rulers; crayons; drawing paper; reproducible, "Attributes and Shapes," for each student.

PROCEDURE

1. Review common shapes and their attributes, as provided in the Background.

2. Hand out the materials. Explain that the reproducible contains the attributes of six shapes. Students are to number, draw, and name each shape, based on the attributes. They may color the shapes.

Check your students' drawings. Have them compare their drawings with those of classmates nearby and discuss similarities and differences. Ask questions such as the following:

- Which shapes that you drew were the same as the shapes others drew?

- Which shapes were different? In what ways were these shapes different? (For example, it is likely that the sizes of shapes varied. It is also likely that the lengths and widths of rectangles varied and that the types of triangles were different.)

ANSWERS

(**1**) Square (**2**) Pentagon (**3**) Hexagon (**4**) Rectangle (**5**) Triangle (**6**) Trapezoid

SHAPE CARDS

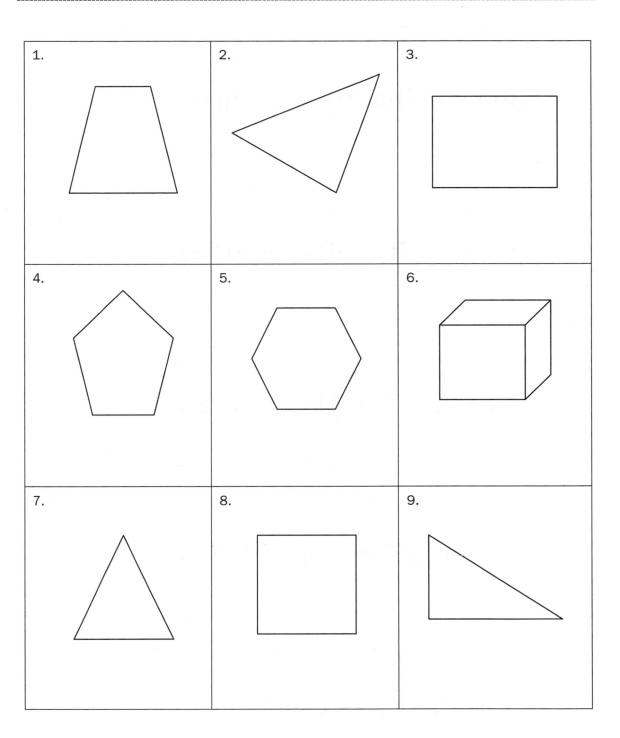

Shapes That Have 3 Angles

Shapes That Have 4 Sides

A Shape That Has 5 Sides

A Shape That Has 6 Sides

A Shape That Has 6 Square Faces

Name _____

ATTRIBUTES AND SHAPES

Directions: Draw each shape. Write the name of each shape next to its drawing.

1. This shape has 4 sides. The sides are the same length. The shape has 4 right angles.

2. This shape has 5 sides and 5 angles.

3. This shape has 6 sides and 6 angles.

4. This shape has 4 sides. Opposite sides are parallel. Opposite sides have the same length. The shape has 4 right angles.

5. This shape has 3 sides and 3 angles.

6. This shape has 4 sides. Only one pair of sides is parallel. The shape has 4 angles.

Geometry: 2.G.2

"Reason with shapes and their attributes."

2. "Partition a rectangle into rows and columns of same-size squares and count to find the total number of them."

BACKGROUND

Rectangles can be partitioned into same-size squares, the number and size of the squares depending on the dimensions of the rectangle. Once students understand this, they have acquired a foundation for working with arrays and area.

ACTIVITY: PARTITIONING RECTANGLES INTO SQUARES

Students will partition rectangles into same-size squares. They will find the total number of squares in each rectangle.

MATERIALS

Rulers with 1-inch and 1-centimeter scales; reproducibles, "A 4-Inch by 5-Inch Rectangle" and "A 7-Centimeter by 10-Centimeter Rectangle," for each student.

PROCEDURE

1. Explain to your students that some shapes can be partitioned, or divided, into same-size squares by dividing them into rows and columns. For an example, sketch a rectangle on the board and partition it by marking off rows and columns. Point out how the rows and columns divide the rectangle into squares that are the same size.

2. Hand out the materials. Explain that each reproducible contains a rectangle. One rectangle is measured in inches and the other is measured in centimeters.

3. Explain that students are to use their rulers and partition the rectangles into rows and columns that result in same-size squares. Students should partition the 4-inch by 5-inch rectangle into 1-inch rows and columns and the 7-centimeter by 10-centimeter rectangle into 1-centimeter rows and columns.

4. Demonstrate how they can divide the rectangles into rows and columns using the ruler with the 1-inch scale for the 4-inch by 5-inch rectangle. Work together as a class and do the following:

   - Place your ruler along the top of the rectangle. Be sure to place the end of the ruler at the end of the line segment.

   - Starting at the end of the line segment, mark a dot at every 1-inch interval.

   - Repeat this procedure on the opposite side.

   - Use your ruler and draw a line from the first dot on one line segment to the first dot directly opposite it on the other line segment.

   - Use your ruler and draw lines to connect the remaining dots.

5. Instruct your students to follow the same procedure with the two other line segments. After they have connected all the pairs of dots, they should have created rows and columns that result in same-size squares. Each square should have 1-inch sides.

6. Tell your students to count the squares and write the total on the line below the rectangle.

7. Instruct your students to follow the same procedure to find the total number of same-size squares in the 7-centimeter by 10-centimeter rectangle. Remind them to use the ruler with the 1-centimeter scale.

CLOSURE

Ask your students what they found to be the total number of same-size squares for each rectangle. (20 squares for the 4-inch by 5-inch rectangle. 70 squares for the 7-centimeter by 10-centimeter rectangle.) Ask: How would partitioning the rectangles into smaller squares change the number of squares? (There would be more squares.) How would partitioning the rectangles into larger squares change the number of squares? (There would be fewer squares.)

A 4-INCH BY 5-INCH RECTANGLE

Directions: Use your ruler to divide the rectangle into 1-inch squares.

Count the squares. The total is _____.

A 7-CENTIMETER BY 10-CENTIMETER RECTANGLE

Directions: Use your ruler to divide the rectangle into 1-centimeter squares.

Count the squares. The total is _____.

Geometry: 2.G.3

"Reason with shapes and their attributes."

> 3. "Partition circles and rectangles into two, three, or four equal shares, describe the shares using the words *halves, thirds, half of, a third of*, etc., and describe the whole as two halves, three thirds, four fourths. Recognize that equal shares of identical wholes need not have the same shape."

BACKGROUND

Understanding that shapes can be partitioned into equal parts is a prerequisite skill for working with fractions. Introducing terminology such as *halves, thirds, wholes*, and so on provides students with the vocabulary to describe geometric figures and their parts and can later be extended to describe quantities.

 ## ACTIVITY 1: PARTITIONING AND DESCRIBING PARTS OF RECTANGLES

Working in pairs or groups of three, students will partition rectangles into halves, thirds, and fourths. They will use appropriate terms to describe the parts of the rectangles.

MATERIALS

Scissors; reproducibles, "Rectangles and Equal Parts, I," "Rectangles and Equal Parts, II," and "Describing Rectangles and Equal Parts," for each pair or group of students.

PROCEDURE

1. Explain that rectangles can be divided into equal parts. Depending on how many parts the rectangle is divided into, a part may be a half of the whole, a third of the whole, a fourth of the whole, and so on. Review the following words: *half, halves, a half of, third, thirds, a third of, fourth, fourths,* and *a fourth of*.

2. To help your students understand that equal shares of identical wholes need not have the same shape, provide the following demonstration:

   - Start with a blank sheet of $8\frac{1}{2}$- by 11-inch paper. Hold it so that a shorter side is on top. Fold the paper in half from top to bottom and ask your students what part of the paper is showing. (Students should recognize that a half is showing.)

- Take another sheet of paper of equal size and hold it so that a longer side is on top. Fold the paper in half from top to bottom and ask your students what part of the paper is showing. (They should recognize that a half is showing.)

- Hold the folded sheets of paper side by side. Ask your students what they can conclude from the size and shape of the rectangles. (They should realize that the rectangles have the same size because they are both a half of the same-sized blank sheets of paper. Students should see that the rectangles are not the same shape.) Emphasize that halves of figures of the same size need not have the same shape.

3. Hand out the materials. Explain that two of the reproducibles contain rectangles. Each rectangle is numbered in the top left corner. Each also has dotted lines that students are to use to divide the rectangles into equal parts. The third reproducible, "Describing Rectangles and Equal Parts," contains statements that students must complete, using the words in the Word Box. If necessary, review the meanings of the words. Some words will be used more than once.

4. Explain that students are to first cut out each rectangle. They are to then fold each rectangle along its dotted lines to divide the rectangle into parts. After they have folded the rectangles into parts, they should open them and use them to complete the statements on the reproducible "Describing Rectangles and Equal Parts."

CLOSURE

Discuss your students' answers. Be sure that your students were able to divide the rectangles into parts correctly.

ANSWERS

Rectangle 1:	(1) half	(2) halves
Rectangle 2:	(1) three	(2) third
Rectangle 3:	(1) fourths	(2) four
Rectangle 4:	(1) half	(2) equal
Rectangle 5:	(1) thirds	(2) equal
Rectangle 6:	(1) fourth	(2) four

ACTIVITY 2: PARTITIONING AND DESCRIBING PARTS OF CIRCLES

Students will partition circles into equal parts. They will use appropriate terms to describe the parts of the circles.

Crayons; reproducibles, "Circles and Equal Parts, I," "Circles and Equal Parts, II," and "Circles and Equal Parts, III," for each student.

PROCEDURE

1. Explain that circles can be divided into equal parts. Together the parts make 1 whole. Review words such as the following: *half, halves, third, thirds, fourth,* and *fourths*.

2. Hand out the materials. Explain that the reproducible contains three circles. Each circle is numbered and is divided into sections labeled with a color. Students are to color each section according to its label.

3. After students have completed coloring the circles, ask them questions such as the following:

   • How many parts is circle 1 divided into? (Two) What part of circle 1 is blue? (A half) What part is green? (A half) What do the two halves of the circle equal? (One whole)

   • What part of circle 2 is yellow? (A third) How many equal parts is circle 2 divided into? (Three) Each part is what part of the whole? (A third) How many thirds make a whole? (Three)

   • How many parts is circle 3 divided into? (Four) What part of the circle is red? (A fourth) What part of the circle is red and green? (A half) What do the blue, green, yellow, and red parts of the circle form? (Four fourths or one whole)

CLOSURE

Review the meanings of the terms: *whole, half, third, fourth, halves, thirds,* and *fourths*. Ask where students have heard these terms before, outside of school.

1.

2.

3.

4.

5.

6.

DESCRIBING RECTANGLES AND EQUAL PARTS

Directions: Answer the questions. Use the words in the Word Box. Some words will be used more than once.

RECTANGLE 1

1) Each part is a _____ of the rectangle.

2) Two _____ equal the whole rectangle.

RECTANGLE 2

1) This rectangle is divided into _____ parts.

2) Each part is a _____ of the whole.

RECTANGLE 3

1) This rectangle is divided into _____.

2) The whole is made up of _____ fourths.

Word Box
equal
half
fourth
third
three
thirds
fourths
halves
four

RECTANGLE 4

1) Each part is a _____ of the whole.

2) Rectangle 1 is the same size as Rectangle 4. The sizes of the parts of these rectangles are _____.

RECTANGLE 5

1) This rectangle is divided into _____.

2) Rectangle 5 is the same size as Rectangle 2. The sizes of the parts of these rectangles are _____.

RECTANGLE 6

1) Each part of this rectangle is a _____ of the whole.

2) The rectangle is divided into _____ equal parts.

1.

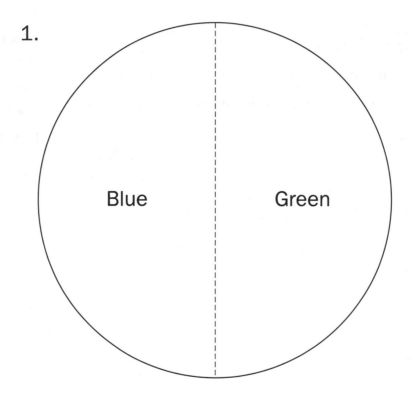

2.

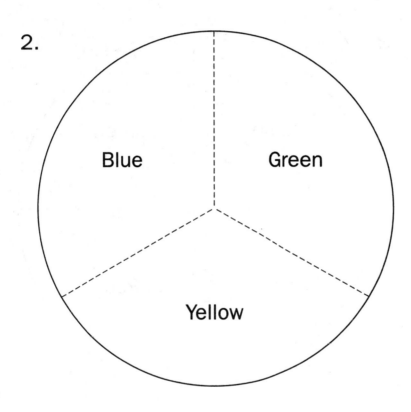

Blue   Green

Yellow

3.

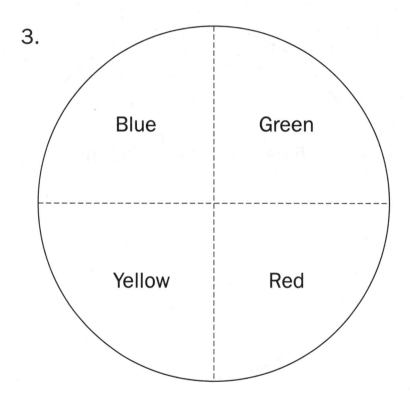

INDEX

work with time and money (Grade 2) using a, 231–233

Analyzing and Comparing Three-Dimensional Shapes activity (Kindergarten), 74–75

Analyzing and Comparing Two-Dimensional Shapes activity (Kindergarten), 72–73

Attribute Cards form (Grade 2), 250

Attributes: describe and compare measurable, 54–57; description of a defining, 150; distinguish between defining versus non-defining, 150–153; recognize and draw shapes having specified, 246–251

Attributes and Shapes form (Grade 2), 251

Axelrod, Amy, 235

B

Bar graphs: constructing, 243–245; description of, 243

Base Ten. *See* Number and operations in Base Ten

Bingo Problems—Adding and Subtracting Within 100 form (Grade 2), 196

A Book About an Even-Numbered Day activity (Grade 2), 175

A Book About Lines and Shapes activity, 150–151

A Book About Math and Money activity (Grade 2), 235–236

A Book About Telling Time activity (Grade 1), 144

Book resources: *Mission: Addition* (Leedy), 110; *My Even Day* (Fisher and Sneed), 175; *Pigs Will Be Pigs* (Axelrod), 235; *Richard Scarry's Best Counting Book Ever* (Scarry), 2; *Telling Time: How to Tell Time on Digital and Analog Clocks!* (Older), 144; *12 Ways to Get to 11* (Merriam), 36; *When a Line Bends . . . A Shape Begins* (Greene), 150

C

Cardinality and counting: compare numbers, 22–26; know number names and count sequence, 2–13; to tell the number of objects, 14–21

Categories, classify and count objects in each, 58–59

Circle form (Grade 1), 161

Circles: correctly name regardless of size or orientation, 62–66; identify and describe, 60–61; identify as two- or three-dimensional, 67–71; partition into two, three, or four equal shares, 257, 262–264; partition into equal shares, 158–161

Circles and Equal Parts form (Grade 2), 262–264

Clay modeling activity (Kindergarten), 78–79

Clocks: tell and write time (Grade 1) using, 144–145; work with time and money (Grade 2) using, 231–234

Coloring Addition and Subtraction Problems form (Kindergarten), 48

Combining Shapes activity (Kindergarten), 80–81

Comparing Attributes of Objects activity (Kindergarten), 56–57

Comparing Numbers activity (Kindergarten), 25–26

Comparing Numbers form (Kindergarten), 24

Comparing Numbers Through 999 activity (Grade 2), 190–191

Comparing Objects and Numbers activity (Kindergarten), 22–23

Cones: correctly name regardless of size or orientation, 62–66; identify and describe, 60–61; identify as two- or three-dimensional, 67–71

Constructing Number Line Diagrams to Show Addition and Subtraction activity (Grade 2), 226–228

Constructing Picture Graphs and Bar Graphs activity (Grade 2), 243–245

Count On: Add or Subtract form (Grade 1), 104

Count sequence: count forward from given number within known, 5–9; count numbers from 0 to 20, 10–13; count to 100 by ones and by tens, 2–4; count to 120, starting at any number less than 120 to extend the, 120–122

Counting: for comparing numbers, 22–26; know number names and the count sequence, 2–13; object classifying, sorting, and, 58–59; relate counting to addition and subtraction, 101–104; to tell the number of objects, 14–21; within 1,000 by 5s, 10s, and 100s, 183–186

Counting and cardinality (Kindergarten): count forward from given number within know count sequence, 5–9; count to 100 by ones and by tens, 2–4; count to answer "how many?" questions, 20–21; identity and compare number of objects in different groups, 22–24; relationship between numbers and quantities and connecting counting to cardinality, 14–21; write numbers from 0 to 20, 10–13

Counting Floor Tiles activity (Kindergarten), 3

Counting Forward and Backward activity (Grade 1), 101–102

The Counting Game activity (Grade 2), 183–184

Counting Game Answer Sheet form (Grade 2), 186

Counting Game Cards form (Grade 2), 185

Counting Number Grid form (Grade 1), 103

H

I

K

L

Leedy, Loreen, 130

Length: add and subtract whole numbers that represent, 226–230; estimate using units of inches, feet, centimeters, and meters, 217–219; measure an object using appropriate tools, 211–213; relate addition and subtraction to, 223–230

Length units: compare different lengths and express difference in terms of, 220–222; estimate length using units of inches, feet, centimeters, and meters, 217–219; express the length of an object as whole number of, 142–143; measure an object twice using two different, 214–217; measuring string in, 142–143; ordering and comparing objects by, 139–142

Lengths form (Grade 1), 141

Line plots: description and example of, 239; Measurement and Line Plots activity (Grade 2), 239–242

M

Making a Three-Dimensional Shape activity (Grade 1), 155–156

Making 10 activity (Kindergarten), 39–40

Making Addition Problems activity (Grade 2), 197–198

Making Models activity (Kindergarten), 78–79

Making Two-Dimensional Shapes activity (Grade 1), 154–155

Matching Time Cards activity (Grade 2), 232

Measurement and data (Kindergarten): classify objects and count objects in each category, 58–59; describe and compare measurable attributes, 54–57

Measurement and data (Grade 1): measure lengths, 139–143; represent and interpret data, 146–149; tell and write time, 144–145

Measurement and data (Grade 2): estimate lengths using units of inches, feet, centimeters, and meters, 217–219; measure length of an object using appropriate tool, 211–213; measure length of an object twice using length units of different lengths, 214–216; measure to compare length of two different objects, 220–222; relate addition and subtraction to length, 223–230; work with time and money, 231–238

Measurement and Line Plots (Grade 2), 239–241

Measurement Recording Sheet form (Grade 2), 213

Measurement Word Problems Within 100 form (Grade 2), 225

Measurements and Length Units activity, 214–215

Measuring Objects with the Appropriate Tools activity (Grade 2), 211–212

Measuring String in Length Units activity (Grade 1), 142–143

Mental Math 100 to 900 Score Sheet form (Grade 2), 208

Mental Math Cards 100 to 900 form (Grade 2), 206

Mental Math Cards 10 and 100 form (Grade 2), 207

Mental Math Game Cards form (Grade 2), 173

Mental Math Game for Adding and Subtracting Within 20 activity (Grade 2), 171–172

Mental Math Game Score Sheet (Grade 2), 174

Mental Math Go Around activity (Grade 2), 204–205

Merriam, Eve, 36

Mini-Math Skit activity (Kindergarten), 29

Miniature Math Bingo activity (Kindergarten), 10–11

Miniature Math Bingo form (Kindergarten), 13

Missing Numbers and Objects form (Kindergarten), 19

Mission: Addition (Leedy), 130

Money measures (Grade 2): A Book about Math and Money activity, 235–236; Money Problems form, 238; The Money Quiz Game activity, 236–237

Money Problems form (Grade 2), 238

The Money Quiz Game activity (Grade 2), 236–237

My Even Day (Fisher and Sneed), 175

N

Names and Shapes, I form (Kindergarten), 65

Names and Shapes, II form (Kindergarten), 66

Number and operations in Base Ten (Kindergarten): Numbers: Tens and Ones, I form, 51; Numbers: Tens and Ones, II form, 52; Numbers: Tens and Ones, III form, 53; Tens and Ones activity, 49–50

Number and operations in Base Ten (Grade 1): extend the counting sequence, 120–122; use place value operations to add and subtract, 130–138; understand place value, 123–129

Number and operations in Base Ten (Grade 2): add and subtract within 1,000 using place value and operation properties, 200–203; add up to four two-digit numbers using place value and operation properties, 197–199; explain why addition and subtraction strategies work using place value and operation properties, 209–210; mentally add or subtract 10 or 100 to given number 99–900, 204–208; use place value to fluently add and subtract within 100, 193–196; understand place value, 180–192

Number Line Diagrams—Addition and Subtraction form (Grade 2), 229

Number Set, I form (Kindergarten), 8

Number Set, II form (Kindergarten), 9

Numbers: adding up to four two-digit, 197–199; compare two three-digit, 190–192; comparing, 22–26; count from 0 to 20, 10–13; count to 100 by ones and by tens, 2–4; count within 1,000 by 5s, 10s, and 100s, 183–186; creating three-digit, 180–182; decomposing by adding and subtracting, 36–38; filling in objects and, 15–16, 19; identifying count of objects using, 14–21; know count sequence and names of, 2–13; pairing objects and, 14–15, 17–18; read and write to 1,000 using base-ten numerals, number names, and expanded form, 187–189. *See also* Unknown numbers; Whole numbers

Numbers: Tens and Ones, I form (Kindergarten), 51

Numbers: Tens and Ones, II form (Kindergarten), 52

Numbers: Tens and Ones, III form (Kindergarten), 53

Numbers and Grids activity (Grade 1), 123–124

Numbers and Objective activity (Kindergarten), 11–12

Numbers for Making Addition Problems form (Grade 2), 199

Numbers-Objects Cards, I form (Kindergarten), 17

Numbers-Objects Cards, II form (Kindergarten), 18

Numbers War Game activity (Grade 1), 127–128

Numbers War Game Score Sheet form (Grade 1), 129

O

Objects: addition and subtraction word problems using, 86–91; addition of numbers to make 10 when added to given number using, 39–42; classify and counted in each category, 58–59; comparing numbers of, 22–24; count to 120 and use numeral to represent, 120–122; counting to tell the number of, 14–21; decomposing numbers using, 36–38; describe and compare measurable attributes of, 54–57; express the length as whole number of length unit, 142–143; filling in numbers and, 15–16, 19; gain foundations for multiplication by

working with equal groups or, 175–179; measure and estimate lengths in standard units, 211–222; ordering and comparing length of, 139–142; pairing numbers and, 14–15, 17–18; representing addition and subtraction using, 27–32; Spilling Objects activity (Grade 2), 176. *See also* Data representation and interpretation

Older, Jules, 144

100-Unit Grids form (Grade 1), 126

Operations and algebraic thinking (Kindergarten): addition of numbers to make 10 when added to the given number, using objects or drawings, 39–42; decompose numbers less than or equal to 10 into pairs, 36–38; find the number that makes 10 when added to the given number, 39–42; fluently add and subtract within 5, 43–48; represent addition and subtraction objects, images, sounds, verbals, or equations, 27–32; representations of addition and subtraction, 27–35; solve addition and subtraction word problems, 33–35

Operations and algebraic thinking (Grade 1): add and subtract within 20, 105–111; add and subtract within 20 to solve word problems with unknown numbers, 86–91; apply properties of operations as strategies to add and subtract, 95–97; determine unknown whole number in equation relating three whole numbers, 116–119; relate counting to addition and subtraction, 101–104; solve work problems involving addition and subtraction, 92–94; understand meaning of the equal sign, 112–115; understand subtraction as an unknown-addend problem, 98–100

Operations and algebraic thinking (Grade 2): addition and subtraction within 100 to work problems, 164–165; fluently add and subtract within 20 using mental strategies, 171–174; work with equal groups or objects to gain foundations for multiplication, 175–179

Ordering and Comparing Objects by Length activity (Grade 1), 139–140

P

Pairing Numbers and Objects activity (Kindergarten), 14–15

Partitioning and Describing Parts of Circle activity (Grade 2), 257–258

Partitioning and Describing Parts of Rectangles activity (Grade 2), 256–257

Partitioning Circles activity (Grade 1), 158–159

W

When a Line Bends. . .A Shape Begins (Greene), 150

Whole numbers: add and subtract lengths represented by, 226–230; determining unknown whole number in equation, 116–119; express the length of an object as length unit of, 142–143; solve word problems adding three whole numbers less than 20, 92–94. *See also* Numbers

Word Box form (Grade 2), 261

Word problems: addition and subtraction within 100 to solve, 164–170; involving dollar bills and coins of different values, 235–238; solving addition and subtraction (Kindergarten), 33–35; solving addition with unknown numbers (Grade 1), 86–94; solving measurement-related, 223–225; solving subtraction with unknown numbers (Grade 1), 92–94

Word Problems—Adding To and Taking From activity (Grade 1), 86–87

Word Problems (Adding To and Taking From) form (Grade 2), 168

Word Problems Involving Adding To and Taking From activity (Grade 2), 164–165

Word Problems Involving Putting Together, Taking Apart, and Comparing activity (Grade 2), 166–167

Word Problems—Putting Together, Taking Apart, and Comparing activity (Grade 1), 87–88

Word Problems (Putting Together, Taking Apart, and Comparing) form (Grade 2), 169

Word Problems with Adding and Subtracting form, 35

Word Problems with Three Addends activity (Grade 1), 92–94

Working with Data activity (Grade 1), 146–147